10-MINUTE
BRAIN GAMES
WORDS AND LANGUAGE

Michael O'Mara Books Limited

First published in Great Britain in 2018 by
Michael O'Mara Books Limited
9 Lion Yard
Tremadoc Road
London SW4 7NQ

A CIP catalogue record for this book is available from the British Library.

Papers used by Michael O'Mara Books Limited are natural, recyclable
products made from wood grown in sustainable forests. The manufacturing
processes conform to the environmental regulations of the country of
origin.

ISBN: 978-1-78243-906-6 in paperback print format

1 2 3 4 5 6 7 8 9 10

www.mombooks.com
www.drgarethmoore.com

Designed and typeset by Gareth Moore
Printed and bound by CPI Group (UK) Ltd, Croydon, CR0 4YY

▪ Introduction ▪

Welcome to *10-Minute Brain Games: Words and Language*, packed from cover to cover with many different types of word and language puzzle, all designed to be solvable in around 10 minutes or so.

Full instructions for every puzzle are conveniently located at the bottom of each page, with a sentence or paragraph to give the basic aim and then some bullet points to specify the finer rules of that particular type, if necessary.

There's a handy area on each page for keeping track of your solving time, which you may well find will vary quite significantly from puzzle type to puzzle type. Each type of puzzle appears six or seven times throughout the book, however, so if you note down your times you can then discover if you get any faster at particular types as you work through the book.

The 10-minute time is simply a general target, and you may well find that you take longer than this on some puzzles. Keep going until you're finished on those puzzles, or if you're stuck then sneak a hint from the solutions at the back of the book. These solutions are also useful for checking your answers, should you wish to.

Good luck, and have fun!

▪ Word Pyramid ▪

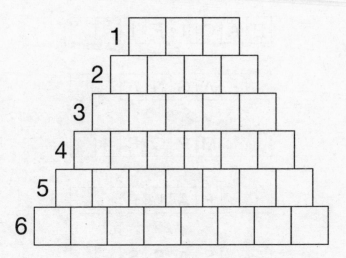

1 Current unit
2 Tropical tree
3 Ornamental tree
4 Specimen
5 Pierces
6 Lose

Instructions

Solve each clue and write the answer into the corresponding row of the pyramid.

• Each row of the pyramid contains the same set of letters as the row above it, plus one extra. The letters may be in a different order, however.

▪ Zigzag ▪

| P | A | C | I | F | I | | |

| | | A | G | N | A | | |

| | | M | P | O | R | | |

| | | F | A | L | F | | |

| | | S | A | S | S | | |

| | | N | U | E | N | | |

| | | C | U | M | E | N | T |

Instructions

Write a letter in each grey box so that every line contains an eight-letter word.

- Each pair of grey boxes is linked to another pair of grey boxes. Each linked pair contains the same two letters, in the same relative positions.

Your solving time: _____

▪ Fit Word ▪

3 Letters
Ash
Bee
Cos
Elm
Fir
Fur
Goo
Irk
Keg
Maw
Nil
Ohm
Old

Owe
Paw
Pro
Rag
Rep
Sue
Sum
Tap
Tic
Via

4 Letters
Four
Kite

Mega
Ping
Tofu
Used

5 Letters
Alike
Baths
Ebony
Fills
Totem
Trunk

6 Letters
Floats
Marker
Ravage
Strike

7 Letters
Encoded
Satanic

Instructions

Enter each of the listed words into the grid, one letter per square. Each word should read either across or down.

Your solving time: _____

▪ **Word Chains** ▪

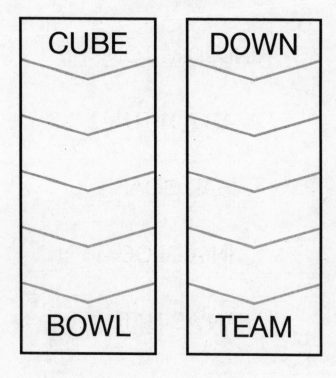

CUBE

BOWL

DOWN

TEAM

Instructions

Complete each of these two word chains by writing a four-letter word into each gap. Once complete, the top word of each chain should link to the bottom word in five steps.

• Each word must use the same letters in the same order as the word above, but with just one letter changed.

Your solving time: _____

▪ Anagrams ▪

KIND, DIM TONGUE

AS A RITUAL

BAD BOARS

IN A GLOOM

FAN AS HATING

Instructions

Each of the above is an anagram of a country. Can you unscramble each set of letters?

▪ **Encrypted Quote** ▪

"Mj csyv egxmsrw mrwtmvi
sxlivw xs hvieq qsvi, xs pievr
qsvi, hs qsvi erh figsqi qsvi,
csy evi e piehiv."

– Nslr Uymrgc Eheqw

Instructions

The text above contains an encrypted historical quote.

• Each letter in the text has been shifted by a constant
amount, so for example if the shift was up by two places
then A would have been changed to C, and B to D, and C to
E, and so on through until X to Z, and Y to A, and Z to B.

▪ Crossword ▪

Across
1 Extents (6)
4 Rappel (6)
8 Large, flightless bird (3)
9 Twin-hulled boat (9)
11 Youths (4)
12 Set apart for special use (8)
15 Admired (9)
18 Tasks to be done (8)
19 Sonic the Hedgehog company (4)
21 Police facial image aid (9)
23 Talk fondly (3)
24 Oily (6)
25 Jail (6)

Down
1 Intensely (6)
2 Pillager (9)
3 Meat knuckle (4)
5 Have a chance encounter with (4,4)
6 A talent for music or language (3)
7 Key part of spectacles (6)
10 Amusement ground (5,4)
13 Groups of spectators (9)
14 Separates (8)
16 Possessing (6)
17 Abandon, as on an island (6)
20 Mix a liquid (4)
22 Ogle (3)

Instructions

Solve each clue and write the answer into the grid, one letter per square. Write either across or down as indicated.

Your solving time: _____

▪ **Vowelless** ▪

M ZN

RG RN D

T HM S

R NC

G NGS

Instructions

All of the vowels have been removed from the famous rivers above. Can you restore them to reveal the original words?

• Any existing spaces have been removed, and then some random spaces have been added to make it a little trickier.

Your solving time: _____

▪ Word Circle ▪

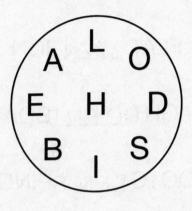

_____

_____

_____

_____

_____

_____

Instructions

How many words can you find in the word circle above?

- Every word must use the centre letter, plus at least two others.
- There is one word that uses every letter.

There are at least 60 words to be found.

▪ Link Words ▪

FLAT _ _ _ _ ION

NIGHT _ _ _ _ BOAT

BOOTS _ _ _ _ PINGS

HONEY _ _ _ _ BEAM

SNOW _ _ _ _ _ WOOD

Instructions

Find a common English word to place in each gap, so that you make two new words – one when you join that word to the end of the first word, and one when you join that word to the start of the second word.

• For example, 'birth _ _ _ break' could be solved using 'day', making birthday and daybreak.

Your solving time: _____

▪ Codeword ▪

		4		6		8		4		6		24	N
A												
B	4	6	16	4	19	4		22	5 U	3	12	10	O
C		8		3		20	6	5		26		4	P
D	1	26	10	4	26	13		4	17	4	3	6	Q
E	8			7			16		3		20		R
F	10	11	8	12	3	19		4	17	10	26	9	S
G| 9		5			6	8	16			13		9	T
H|	25	26	8	7	4		4	9	6	10	10	16	U
I|	8		7		13				10			10	V
J| 18	3	12	10	26			15	3	2	9	4 A	14	W
K	5		14		4	26	25		20		10		X
L	9	7	3	20	20		3	7	20	4	23	13	Y
M	21		7		12		7		13		3		Z

1	2	3	4	5	6	7	8	9	10	11	12	13
14	15	16	17	18	19	20	21	22	23	24	25	26

Instructions

Solve this coded crossword in which every letter has been replaced by a number, indicated by the small digits in the top-left corner of each square.

- Work out which number represents each letter of the alphabet, and use this information to complete the grid.
- Keep track of the code by using the boxes beneath the puzzle, and the used letters with the letters outside the grid.

Your solving time: _____

▪ Spiral Crossword ▪

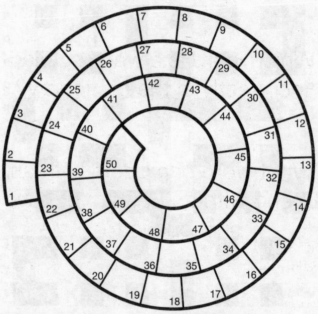

Inward

1-7 Contrives to obtain
8-12 VII, to the Romans
13-17 Inner self
18-21 Paving stone
22-24 Rotate a helicopter
25-27 Letter after zeta
28-35 Snatching
36-39 Possible hair infestation
40-46 Against
47-50 Scored 100% on

Outward

50-45 Rosary division
44-42 Easy concession
41-35 Mailing
34-32 Pen tip
31-29 Drinks counter
28-22 Entrance
21-16 Aromatic ointment
15-11 Absurd
10-5 Ship
4-1 Chew like a beaver

Instructions

Solve the clues and write the answers in the given direction.

Your solving time: _____

▪ Word Riddles ▪

Which word is always spelled incorrectly in the dictionary?

What word can begin with an E, end with an E, and yet have only one letter?

Instructions

Can you solve both of the riddles above?

- The riddles work by using word plays, e.g. by deliberately using a different meaning of a word to that expected.

▪ Arrow Word ▪

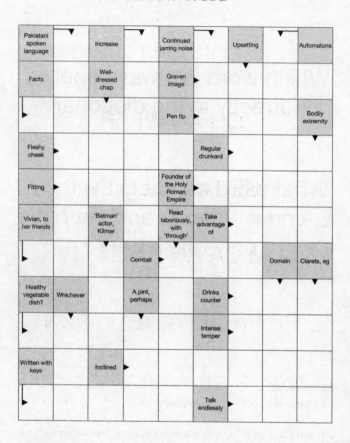

Instructions

Solve this crossword in which all of the clues are given within the grid.

• Each arrow points to where the answer should be written.

Your solving time: _____

▪ Deleted Pairs ▪

OR AW LH

QH AU WI KR

SE TA GC LO ER

CM OA RN SA RV GY

PR EA NM AG BU AI DN

Instructions

Delete one letter from each pair in order to reveal a set of five birds.

- For example, given DC RO LG you could cross out the C, R and L to leave DOG: D~C~ ~R~O ~L~G.

▪ Every Second Letter ▪

_E_A_U_

_R_A _I_O_

_A_I_T_R_U_

_A_U_R_U_

_A_S_O_E_A

Instructions

Can you identify all five of these constellations?

• Every other letter has been removed from each word, so 'example' could have been written as either E_A_P_E or as _X_M_L_.

■ Word Square ■

E	C	R	E
S	U	S	T
R	N	E	A
E	D	I	R

_____

_____

_____

_____

_____

Instructions

How many words can you find in the word square above?

- Spell each word by starting on any letter and then moving left/right/up/down to adjacent letters, without revisiting any square within a word.
- There is one word that uses every letter.

There are at least 40 words to be found.

■ First and Last ■

GEND

AUSTI

TUDIO

OCA

_AI_

Instructions

The same letter has been removed from the start and end of each word above, with a different letter for each word.

• Identify the missing letter for each line, and restore the original words.

Your solving time: _____

■ A-Z Crossword ■

A B C D E F G H I J K L M
N O P Q R S T U V W X Y Z

Instructions

Complete this crossword grid so that each horizontal and vertical run of white squares spells a word.

- Each letter from A to Z is missing exactly once from the grid.
- Use the letters beneath the grid to keep track of which letters are remaining to be placed.

▪ Starting Sequences ▪

MVEMJS

FSTFFS

TPM AOTC ROTS ANH TESB
ROTJ TFA

Instructions

Can you identify each of the sequences above, and then say what letter, or set of letters, should come next?

- The first letters of words or names are given.
- Each sequence is based on either general knowledge or on word meanings. For example, M T W T F S would be followed by Sunday since these are the days of the week: Monday, Tuesday, Wednesday, Thursday, Friday, Saturday, Sunday.

Your solving time: _____

■ Greek Mythology Word Search ■

```
C A C R S U L C O R T A P S Y
C N A T H E R C U L E S H M E
C H D H T S E O A S U D E M P
L N M T S H S S D I S T C A O
S O U E B A E U U Y S N T I L
E N S L E           S T O R E
L M S E A           A S R P N
L E E M T           R C E O E
I M D A A           S E I U P
H A E C L           A H P L S
C G M H A I S I E L O U N E A
A A O U N C I R M L C P T A J
L E I S T R R E N E I Y H S A
L P D L A A B N O S A J C O X
H E L E N N O S P Y L A C A N
```

ACHILLES	CYCLOPS	ODYSSEUS
AGAMEMNON	DIOMEDES	PATROCLUS
AJAX	HECTOR	PENELOPE
ARGONAUTS	HELEN	PERSEUS
ATALANTA	HERCULES	PRIAM
BELLEROPHON	ICARUS	SIRENS
BRISEIS	JASON	TELEMACHUS
CADMUS	MEDUSA	THESEUS
CALYPSO	NARCISSUS	

Instructions

Find all these entries in the grid, in any direction. The middle of the grid is missing and must be restored.

Your solving time: _____

▪ Mixed Pairs ▪

DACONZFEUSDED

THLEOLUIMSAE

BOCLNNYIDEE

ANCLTEOOPANTYRA

BTHUESTUNDCHANCCAESSKIIDDY

Instructions

Five film titles are given, each of which consists of two parts separated by 'and'. The letters from the two parts have then been mixed together, although without changing the order of the letters within either part.

• For example, 'alive and kicking' could be written as **ALIKIVCKIENG**, or as **KAILCKIVINEG**.

Your solving time: _____

▪ Letter Soup ▪

Instructions

Can you rearrange these letters to reveal five colours?

- Each letter is used in exactly one of the five answers, and each answer is a single word.

Your solving time: _____

▪ Initial Letters ▪

ACO by SK

CK by OW

SLIH by BW

PF by QT

LIT by SC

Instructions

Can you identify all of these film titles, and their associated directors?

• Only the initial letters of each title and director are given.

Your solving time: _____

▪ Word Pyramid ▪

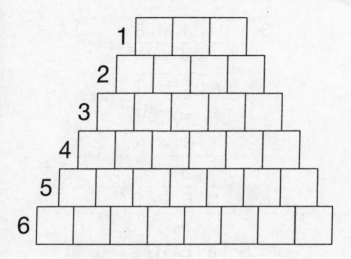

1 Area plan
2 Slope between levels
3 Painful contraction
4 Tent user
5 Run lightly
6 Notes similarities and differences

Instructions
Solve each clue and write the answer into the corresponding row of the pyramid.

- Each row of the pyramid contains the same set of letters as the row above it, plus one extra. The letters may be in a different order, however.

▪ Zigzag ▪

G	L	U	M	M	E		

		A	T	U	T		

		T	R	A	N		

		N	E	R	O		

		E	F	U	L		

		N	C	H	P		

		S	T	A	L	L	S

Instructions

Write a letter in each grey box so that every line contains an eight-letter word.

- Each pair of grey boxes is linked to another pair of grey boxes. Each linked pair contains the same two letters, in the same relative positions.

Your solving time: _____

▪ Fit Word ▪

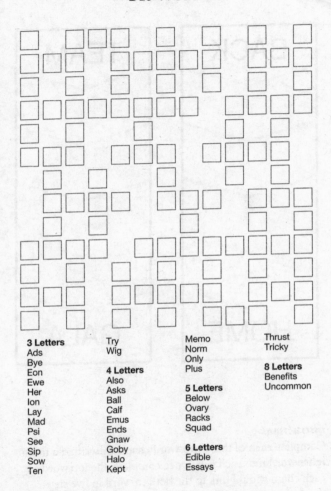

3 Letters	Try	Memo	Thrust
Ads	Wig	Norm	Tricky
Bye		Only	
Eon	**4 Letters**	Plus	**8 Letters**
Ewe	Also		Benefits
Her	Asks	**5 Letters**	Uncommon
Ion	Ball	Below	
Lay	Calf	Ovary	
Mad	Emus	Racks	
Psi	Ends	Squad	
See	Gnaw		
Sip	Goby	**6 Letters**	
Sow	Halo	Edible	
Ten	Kept	Essays	

Instructions

Enter each of the listed words into the grid, one letter per square. Each word should read either across or down.

Your solving time: _____

▪ **Word Chains** ▪

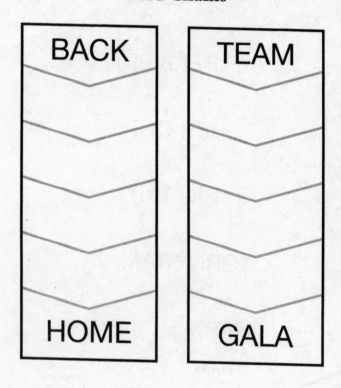

Instructions

Complete each of these two word chains by writing a four-letter word into each gap. Once complete, the top word of each chain should link to the bottom word in five steps.

• Each word must use the same letters in the same order as the word above, but with just one letter changed.

Your solving time: _____

▪ Anagrams ▪

REAR FIR

HER COPS

BIG TAUT

TORN STAMINA

HARM BOILING

Instructions
Each of the above is an anagram of a sports car brand. Can you unscramble each set of letters?

▪ **Encrypted Quote** ▪

"Va znggref bs fglyr, fjvz jvgu gur pheerag; va znggref bs cevapvcyr, fgnaq yvxr n ebpx."

– Gubznf Wrssrefba

Instructions

The text above contains an encrypted historical quote.

- Each letter in the text has been shifted by a constant amount, so for example if the shift was up by two places then A would have been changed to C, and B to D, and C to E, and so on through until X to Z, and Y to A, and Z to B.

Your solving time: _____

▪ Crossword ▪

Across
1 Pace (5)
4 Shocks (7)
9 Italian dessert (8)
10 Visage (4)
11 Owned property (6)
12 Adjusted pitch (5)
13 Baked pastry dishes (4)
15 Type of cereal plant (3)
16 Herds of whales (4)
17 Soft leather made from sheepskin (5)
19 Hidden hacking software (6)
21 'Stop, Rover!' (4)
22 Above the ground (2,3,3)
23 Supplying (7)
24 Heavily built (5)

Down
2 Ways out (5)
3 Heavenly requests (7)
5 Journalism (6,6)
6 Waiflike (5)
7 Came to a conclusion (7)
8 Thesis (12)
14 Convicts (7)
16 Objection (7)
18 Beaver-like rodent (5)
20 Goodbye (5)

Instructions

Solve each clue and write the answer into the grid, one letter per square. Write either across or down as indicated.

Your solving time: _____

▪ Vowelless ▪

G TR

P HN M

PN

MT HR GN

KL L

Instructions

All of the vowels have been removed from the musical instruments above. Can you restore them to reveal the original words?

- Any existing spaces have been removed, and then some random spaces have been added to make it a little trickier.

Your solving time: _____

■ Word Circle ■

_____

_____

_____

_____

_____

Instructions

How many words can you find in the word circle above?

- Every word must use the centre letter, plus at least two others.
- There is one word that uses every letter.

There are at least 90 words to be found.

Your solving time: _____   39

■ Link Words ■

EAST _ _ _ _ ROBE

CAT _ _ _ _ OUT

MOUTH _ _ _ _ _ WORK

PIN _ _ _ _ _ LED

EVERY _ _ _ _ _ UPON

Instructions

Find a common English word to place in each gap, so that you make two new words – one when you join that word to the end of the first word, and one when you join that word to the start of the second word.

• For example, 'birth _ _ _ break' could be solved using 'day', making birthday and daybreak.

　　　　　　　　Your solving time: _____

▪ Codeword ▪

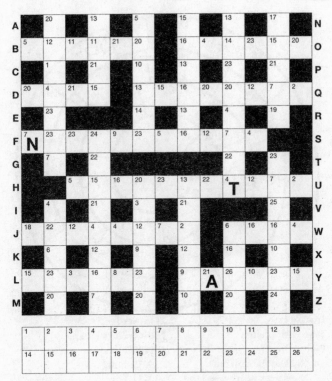

Instructions

Solve this coded crossword in which every letter has been replaced by a number, indicated by the small digits in the top-left corner of each square.

- Work out which number represents each letter of the alphabet, and use this information to complete the grid.
- Keep track of the code by using the boxes beneath the puzzle, and the used letters with the letters outside the grid.

Your solving time: _____

▪ Spiral Crossword ▪

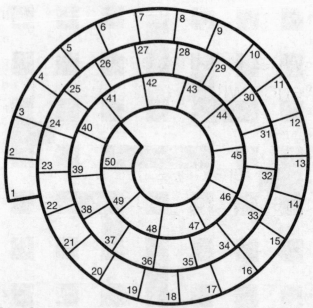

Inward

1-6 Arboretum
7-13 Great joy
14-16 Find the sum of
17-23 Pierces with a weapon
24-26 Pump an accelerator
27-30 Doe and roe, eg
31-35 Brusque
36-39 Solid oils
40-43 Wooded valley
44-46 Qualifiers
47-50 Lively folk dance

Outward

50-46 Dirty looks
45-40 Occupied
39-35 Employees
34-32 Fuzz
31-27 Avarice
26-22 Poetry
21-19 Kiddy seat?
18-13 Noon
12-10 Convened
9-5 Part of a play
4-1 Cross-dressing

Instructions

Solve the clues and write the answers in the given direction.

Your solving time: _____

▪ Word Riddles ▪

What is it that begins with T, ends with T, and is full of T?

Where does five always precede four, three, two and one?

Instructions

Can you solve both of the riddles above?

- The riddles work by using word plays, e.g. by deliberately using a different meaning of a word to that expected.

▪ Arrow Word ▪

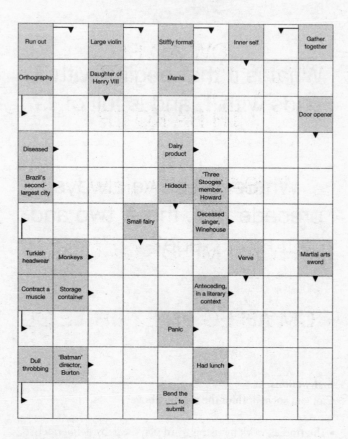

Run out	▼	Large violin	▼	Stiffly formal	▼	Inner self	▼	Gather together
Orthography		Daughter of Henry VIII		Mania ►		▼		
►			▼					Door opener
Diseased ►				Dairy product ►				▼
Brazil's second-largest city ►				Hideout		'Three Stooges' member, Howard ►		
►			Small fairy		Deceased singer, Winehouse ►			
Turkish headwear	Monkeys ►		▼			Verve		Martial arts sword
Contract a muscle	Storage container ►			Anteceding, in a literary context ►		▼		▼
►				Panic ►				
Dull throbbing	'Batman' director, Burton ►				Had lunch ►			
►				Bend the ___, to submit				

Instructions

Solve this crossword in which all of the clues are given within the grid.

• Each arrow points to where the answer should be written.

▪ Deleted Pairs ▪

CW AO BD

TH RA KO ER

SA WH UA IR KL

HY AU MD DP OT CI KC

CM AH EC EK EZ ER TE OL

Instructions

Delete one letter from each pair in order to reveal a set of five fish.

- For example, given DC RO LG you could cross out the C, R and L to leave DOG: DC̶ RO L̶G̶.

Your solving time: _____

▪ Every Second Letter ▪

_N_L_S_

S_A_I_H

_A_D_R_N

_O_T_G_E_E

_U_S_A_

Instructions

Can you identify all five of these languages?

• Every other letter has been removed from each word, so 'example' could have been written as either E_A_P_E or as _X_M_L_.

Your solving time: _____

▪ Starting Sequences ▪

R O Y G B I

K P C O F G

AR CA CO CT DE

sequences above, and then say
hould come next?

ames are given.
her general knowledge or
le, M T W T F S would be
are the days of the week:
Thursday, Friday, Saturday,

lving time: _____

▪ Word Square ▪

I	T	N	U
O	U	C	O
N	T	I	N
A	L	T	S

_____

_____

_____

_____

_____

_____

Instructions
How many words can you find in the word square above?

- Spell each word by starting on any letter and then moving left/right/up/down to adjacent letters, without revisiting any square within a word.
- There is one word that uses every letter.

There are at least 20 words to be found.

▪ First and Last ▪

_RI_

IDO

ULOGIZ

AGE

ARO

Instructions

The same letter has been removed from the start and end of
each word above, with a different letter for each word.

• Identify the missing letter for each line, and restore the
  original words.

Your solving time: _____

▪ A-Z C

Instructions

Can you identify each of the
what letter, or set of letters, s

• The first letters of words or
• Each sequence is based on ei
on word meanings. For examp
followed by Sunday since these
Monday, Tuesday, Wednesday,
Sunday.

50

Your so

Your solving

AL AK AZ

▪ Herbs and Spices Word Search ▪

```
F E V O L C I R E M R U T T I S
S P E P P E R N N O R F F A S R
E B E C D R A T S U M K R U H E
V A E C I P S L L A E A A S W P
I Y M C E L E N N E F C I A W A
H L O A O E S U R E R D S A O C
C E M M L M           A T L N J
P A A U A M           E P G A J
A F D S E N           O A S G U
P D R G E A           R M B E N
R I A F R A           I A P R I
I L C R R O I E Y I N S C R O P
K L A Y H M S H C E I T H Y M E
A T P A R S L E Y L L E T E B R
A N I S E E D O O W M R O W P A
C U M I N R E W O L F R E D L E
```

ALLSPICE	CLOVE	JASMINE	ROSEMARY
ALOE	CUMIN	JUNIPER	SAFFRON
ANISEED	DILL	MINT	SUMAC
BASIL	ELDERFLOWER	MUSTARD	TARRAGON
BAY LEAF	FENNEL	NUTMEG	THYME
BETEL	FENUGREEK	OREGANO	TURMERIC
CAPERS	GARLIC	PAPRIKA	WASABI
CARDAMOM	HORSERADISH	PARSLEY	WATERCRESS
CHIVES	HYSSOP	PEPPER	WORMWOOD

Instructions

Find all these entries in the grid, in any direction. The middle of the grid is missing and must be restored.

Your solving time: _____   51

▪ Mixed Pairs ▪

WPEAARCE

PRPIREJDUDIECE

CPUNRIISHMMEENT

THEOTHLEDMSANEA

THESTHOEFUUNRYD

Instructions

Five classic novels are given, each of which consists of two parts separated by 'and'. The letters from the two parts have then been mixed together, although without changing the order of the letters within either part.

• For example, 'alive and kicking' could be written as **ALIKIVCKIENG**, or as **KAILCKIVINEG**.

Your solving time: _____

▪ **Letter Soup** ▪

Instructions

Can you rearrange these letters to reveal five Greek gods and goddesses?

- Each letter is used in exactly one of the five answers, and each answer is a single word.

▪ Initial Letters ▪

DOAS by AM

RAJ by WS

ASND by TW

WFG by SB

P by GBS

Instructions

Can you identify all of these plays, and their associated playwrights?

• Only the initial letters of each title and playwright are given.

Your solving time: _____

▪ Word Pyramid ▪

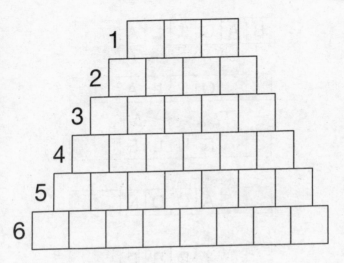

1 Glide over snow
2 x, perhaps
3 Dangers
4 Goes around the edge of
5 Collides with
6 *, perhaps

Instructions

Solve each clue and write the answer into the corresponding row of the pyramid.

- Each row of the pyramid contains the same set of letters as the row above it, plus one extra. The letters may be in a different order, however.

Your solving time: _____

▪ Zigzag ▪

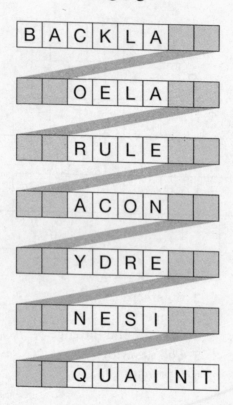

| B | A | C | K | L | A | | |

| | | O | E | L | A | | |

| | | R | U | L | E | | |

| | | A | C | O | N | | |

| | | Y | D | R | E | | |

| | | N | E | S | I | | |

| | | Q | U | A | I | N | T |

Instructions

Write a letter in each grey box so that every line contains an eight-letter word.

- Each pair of grey boxes is linked to another pair of grey boxes. Each linked pair contains the same two letters, in the same relative positions.

Your solving time: _____

▪ Fit Word ▪

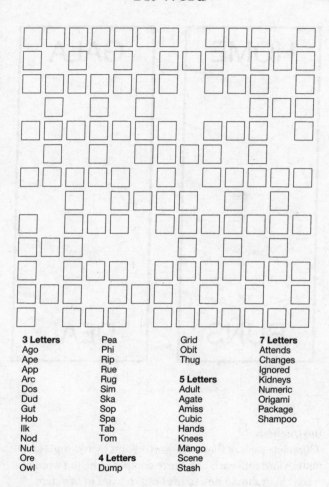

3 Letters	Pea	Grid	7 Letters
Ago	Phi	Obit	Attends
Ape	Rip	Thug	Changes
App	Rue		Ignored
Arc	Rug	5 Letters	Kidneys
Dos	Sim	Adult	Numeric
Dud	Ska	Agate	Origami
Gut	Sop	Amiss	Package
Hob	Spa	Cubic	Shampoo
Ilk	Tab	Hands	
Nod	Tom	Knees	
Nut		Mango	
Ore	4 Letters	Scene	
Owl	Dump	Stash	

Instructions

Enter each of the listed words into the grid, one letter per square. Each word should read either across or down.

Your solving time: _____

▪ Word Chains ▪

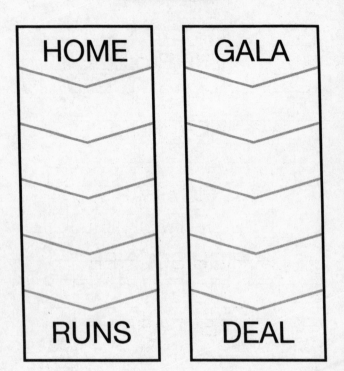

Instructions

Complete each of these two word chains by writing a four-letter word into each gap. Once complete, the top word of each chain should link to the bottom word in five steps.

• Each word must use the same letters in the same order as the word above, but with just one letter changed.

Your solving time: _____

▪ Anagrams ▪

THE PANEL

NEAT POLE

FIG FEAR

RICH SOONER

TENT AREA

Instructions

Each of the above is an anagram of a mammal. Can you
unscramble each set of letters?

▪ **Encrypted Quote** ▪

"Hpndx zskmznnzn ocvo rcdxc xviijo wz kpo dioj rjmyn viy ocvo rcdxc xviijo mzhvdi ndgzio."

– Qdxojm Cpbj

Instructions

The text above contains an encrypted historical quote.

- Each letter in the text has been shifted by a constant amount, so for example if the shift was up by two places then A would have been changed to C, and B to D, and C to E, and so on through until X to Z, and Y to A, and Z to B.

Your solving time: _____

▪ Crossword ▪

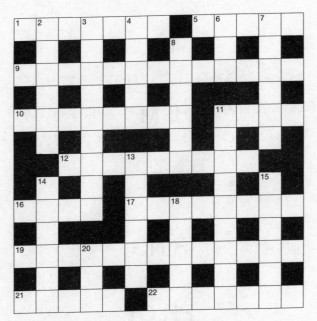

Across
1 Generally speaking (2,1,4)
5 By surprise, as in 'taken ___' (5)
9 Normally (13)
10 Gives advice (8)
11 Powdered grain (4)
12 Election nominee (9)
16 Red, raised mark (4)
17 Took manual control of (8)
19 Ambitious and go-getting (4-9)
21 Sprinkle untidily (5)
22 Mass per unit volume (7)

Down
2 Homily (6)
3 Unemployed (9)
4 Supple (5)
6 Ewe's call (3)
7 Basement (6)
8 Domiciled (6)
11 Component substances (9)
13 Close-harmony rock and roll
   style (3-3)
14 Vanquish (6)
15 Pre-Christmas period (6)
18 Upper classes (5)
20 Entry payment (3)

Instructions

Solve each clue and write the answer into the grid, one letter per square. Write either across or down as indicated.

Your solving time: _____

▪ Vowelless ▪

PR

L M

P PL

R NG

PR CT

Instructions
All of the vowels have been removed from the fruit above. Can you restore them to reveal the original words?

- Any existing spaces have been removed, and then some random spaces have been added to make it a little trickier.

Your solving time: _____

■ Word Circle ■

_____

_____

_____

_____

_____

_____

Instructions

How many words can you find in the word circle above?

- Every word must use the centre letter, plus at least two others.
- There is one word that uses every letter.

There are at least 40 words to be found.

Your solving time: _____   63

■ Link Words ■

POP _ _ _ _ MEAL

SUPER _ _ _ _ _ _ ABLE

OFF _ _ _ BOX

SUN _ _ _ GOING

FORE _ _ _ _ _ _ _ FULLY

Instructions

Find a common English word to place in each gap, so that you make two new words – one when you join that word to the end of the first word, and one when you join that word to the start of the second word.

• For example, 'birth _ _ _ break' could be solved using 'day', making birthday and daybreak.

Your solving time: _____

▪ Codeword ▪

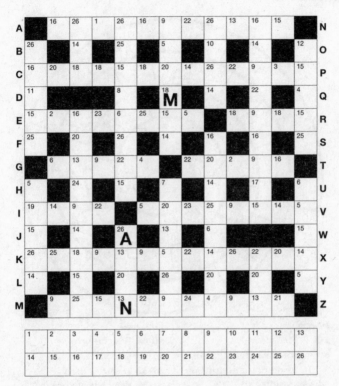

Instructions

Solve this coded crossword in which every letter has been replaced by a number, indicated by the small digits in the top-left corner of each square.

- Work out which number represents each letter of the alphabet, and use this information to complete the grid.
- Keep track of the code by using the boxes beneath the puzzle, and the used letters with the letters outside the grid.

Your solving time: _____

▪ Spiral Crossword ▪

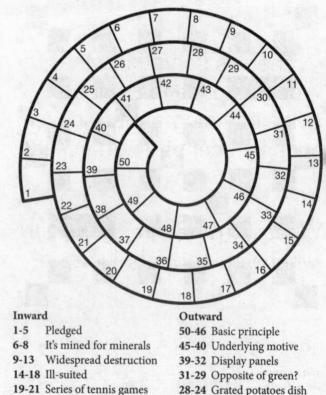

Inward

1-5	Pledged
6-8	It's mined for minerals
9-13	Widespread destruction
14-18	Ill-suited
19-21	Series of tennis games
22-26	Changes a document
27-32	Commands
33-36	Round, griddled bread
37-41	Wanderer
42-47	Nullify
48-50	Ball's target?

Outward

50-46	Basic principle
45-40	Underlying motive
39-32	Display panels
31-29	Opposite of green?
28-24	Grated potatoes dish
23-18	Abhor
17-13	Terror
12-10	Egg cells
9-5	Egret
4-1	Tiers

Instructions

Solve the clues and write the answers in the given direction.

Your solving time: _____

▪ Word Riddles ▪

There is something that occurs once in a minute, twice in a moment but never once in a century. What is it?

What word becomes shorter when you add more letters?

Instructions

Can you solve both of the riddles above?

• The riddles work by using word plays, e.g. by deliberately using a different meaning of a word to that expected.

▪ Arrow Word ▪

Junior	▼	Not requested	▼	Had been	▼	Employee	▼	Coffee dispenser
Animal pelts		Stench		Away from the expected course			▼	
↳		▼		Parent's boy	▶			Lyric poem
Used in fluorescent lamps	▶					Id counterpart	Top-left computer key	▼
Apply styling cream to hair	▶			Consumed frugally: ___ out	▶		▼	
↳								
Type of lapdog		Lost blood		Middle Earth menace	▶			Exploiter
Products	Prefix meaning 'relating to life'	▼		▼		Greasy	Pulitzer Prize winner, Harper	Peron's wife, popularly	▼
↳							▼	▼
Soft, cuddly toy (5,4)	Sand or electric, eg	▶			WALL-E's love	▶		
↳								

Instructions

Solve this crossword in which all of the clues are given within the grid.

• Each arrow points to where the answer should be written.

Your solving time: _____

▪ Deleted Pairs ▪

TJ OU DL OP

AH IO CR KI EC EY

BZ AO XL IL NO GN

QT UE NI DN DI SH

JB UA JS KI ET ST BA MA IL LT

Instructions

Delete one letter from each pair in order to reveal a set of five
sports.

- For example, given DC RO LG you could cross out the C, R
  and L to leave DOG: D̶C̶ ̶R̶O̶ ̶L̶G.

▪ Every Second Letter ▪

E_O_U_

_E_E_I_

_O_A_S

P_A_M_

_U_B_R_

Instructions

Can you identify all five of these books of the Bible?

- Every other letter has been removed from each word, so
  'example' could have been written as either E_A_P_E or as
  _X_M_L_.

Your solving time: _____

▪ Word Square ▪

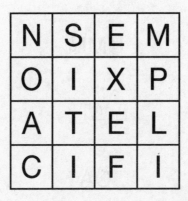

_____

_____

_____

_____

_____

_____

Instructions

How many words can you find in the word square above?

- Spell each word by starting on any letter and then moving left/right/up/down to adjacent letters, without revisiting any square within a word.
- There is one word that uses every letter.

There are at least 20 words to be found.

▪ First and Last ▪

UMM

_WI_

_OA_

RIM

ULA

Instructions

The same letter has been removed from the start and end of each word above, with a different letter for each word.

- Identify the missing letter for each line, and restore the original words.

Your solving time: _____

▪ A-Z Crossword ▪

ABCDEFGHIJKLM
NOPQRSTUVWXYZ

Instructions

Complete this crossword grid so that each horizontal and vertical run of white squares spells a word.

- Each letter from A to Z is missing exactly once from the grid.
- Use the letters beneath the grid to keep track of which letters are remaining to be placed.

Your solving time: _____

▪ Starting Sequences ▪

HHLBBCN

EGEGEVWGGGG

S S QOS CR DAD TWINE

Instructions

Can you identify each of the sequences above, and then say what letter, or set of letters, should come next?

- The first letters of words or names are given.
- Each sequence is based on either general knowledge or on word meanings. For example, M T W T F S would be followed by Sunday since these are the days of the week: Monday, Tuesday, Wednesday, Thursday, Friday, Saturday, Sunday.

Your solving time: _____

▪ Lists Word Search ▪

```
I N T I E S E R I E S T A A E
M T A H E N A S G N E M D L L
C N S L E D U I U Y V N A Y U
A O B I N S S M R B E E R E D
C A N E L M A A E G A O S A E
T R L T E               T L L N H
I A E T E               A M L N C
C N I T B               A T S Y S
L I D A S               S A I R S
Y E C E I               U T T O O
E O A S X I R C E Y A O E L N
V O T G N I T S I L T R U L R
N E S R V N O I T A L U B A T
R U N S D I C T I O N A R Y C
I Y R O T C E R I D T A L L Y
```

AGENDA	INDEX	SCHEDULE
ALMANAC	INVENTORY	SERIES
CALENDAR	ITEMS	SYLLABUS
CHECKLIST	LISTING	TABLE
CONTENTS	REGISTER	TABULATION
DICTIONARY	ROLL	TALLY
DIRECTORY	ROSTER	THESAURUS
ENUMERATION	ROTA	VOCABULARY

Instructions

Find all these entries in the grid, in any direction. The middle of the grid is missing and must be restored.

Your solving time: _____

▪ Mixed Pairs ▪

BAEGCOGNS

MPEOTATOATES

MCACAHEROESNEI

CCHERAECKSERES

SCTRRAEWABEMRRIES

Instructions

Five foods are given, each of which consists of two parts separated by 'and'. The letters from the two parts have then been mixed together, although without changing the order of the letters within either part.

• For example, 'alive and kicking' could be written as **ALIKIVCKIENG**, or as **KAILCKIVINEG**.

Your solving time: _____

▪ Letter Soup ▪

Instructions

Can you rearrange these letters to reveal five cheeses?

• Each letter is used in exactly one of the five answers, and each answer is a single word.

▪ **Initial Letters** ▪

ML by LDV

TSN by VVG

TBOV by SB

GWAPE by JV

TK by GK

Instructions

Can you identify all of the titles of these famous paintings, and their associated artists?

• Only the initial letters of each painting title and artist are given.

Your solving time: _____

▪ Word Pyramid ▪

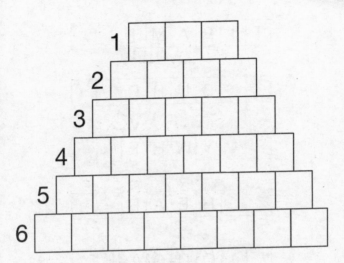

1 Female deer
2 Peaceful bird?
3 Motion recording
4 Entirely lacking
5 Carried to excess
6 Legally dissolved

Instructions

Solve each clue and write the answer into the corresponding row of the pyramid.

- Each row of the pyramid contains the same set of letters as the row above it, plus one extra. The letters may be in a different order, however.

Your solving time: _____

▪ Zigzag ▪

| T | I | R | A | M | I | | |

| | | B | U | R | B | | |

| | | Y | W | H | E | | |

| | | H | E | A | R | | |

| | | Q | U | O | I | | |

| | | T | O | N | I | | |

| | | E | P | H | E | R | D |

Instructions

Write a letter in each grey box so that every line contains an eight-letter word.

- Each pair of grey boxes is linked to another pair of grey boxes. Each linked pair contains the same two letters, in the same relative positions.

Your solving time: _____

▪ Fit Word ▪

3 Letters
Ace
Asp
Cup
Got
Mug
Pat
Pun
Rub
Rum
Sea
Too
Toy
Zoo

4 Letters
Ales
Ashy
Bays
Gaga
Idly
Imps
Pope
Sash
Scan
Tick
Undo
Upon

Visa
Wine

5 Letters
Armed
Assay
Gypsy
Orate
Stoma
Stuns

6 Letters
Addict
Amazes

Entomb
Errors
Milieu
Subtly

Instructions

Enter each of the listed words into the grid, one letter per square. Each word should read either across or down.

Your solving time: _____

▪ Word Chains ▪

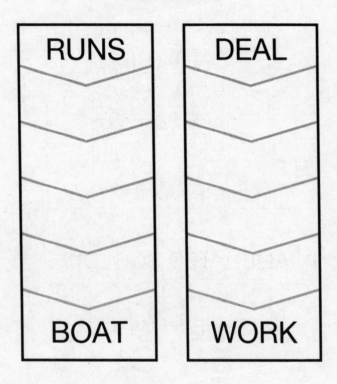

RUNS

BOAT

DEAL

WORK

Instructions

Complete each of these two word chains by writing a four-letter word into each gap. Once complete, the top word of each chain should link to the bottom word in five steps.

• Each word must use the same letters in the same order as the word above, but with just one letter changed.

Your solving time: _____

▪ Anagrams ▪

IN A TRIM

AM THAN ANT

COMPLAINS TOO

ALIENATED SCOLDING

ISSUE IN WRATH

Instructions
Each of the above is an anagram of a cocktail. Can you
unscramble each set of letters?

▪ Encrypted Quote ▪

"Fvb jhu ulcly jyvzz aol vjlhu buaps fvb ohcl aol jvbyhnl av svzl zpnoa vm aol zovyl."

– Joypzavwoly Jvsbtibz

Instructions

The text above contains an encrypted historical quote.

- Each letter in the text has been shifted by a constant amount, so for example if the shift was up by two places then A would have been changed to C, and B to D, and C to E, and so on through until X to Z, and Y to A, and Z to B.

Your solving time: _____

▪ Crossword ▪

Across
1 Popular pastry (6)
4 Electronic dance genre (6)
9 Decreasing in velocity (7)
10 Brings on board (5)
11 Dark stain (4)
12 Ailment (7)
14 Angers (6)
16 Secure against possible loss (6)
19 Cinema film (7)
21 Sprint contest (4)
23 Exactly right (5)
24 Temporarily takes (7)
25 Fears (6)
26 Reduces speed (6)

Down
1 Fading evening light (4)
2 Narrow strips of pasta (7)
3 Key for upper case (5)
5 Organizational level (7)
6 Stallion (5)
7 Preoccupies (8)
8 Another time (5)
13 Provided (8)
15 Untidy, as in hair (7)
17 Expose (7)
18 Words that say what is
   happening (5)
20 Greek island (5)
21 Less common (5)
22 Utilizes (4)

Instructions

Solve each clue and write the answer into the grid, one letter
per square. Write either across or down as indicated.

▪ **Vowelless** ▪

D GS

R PHL

T TN

D VN C

GT T

Instructions

All of the vowels have been removed from the famous artists above. Can you restore them to reveal the original words?

- Any existing spaces have been removed, and then some random spaces have been added to make it a little trickier.

Your solving time: _____

▪ Word Circle ▪

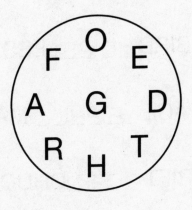

_____

_____

_____

_____

_____

_____

Instructions

How many words can you find in the word circle above?

- Every word must use the centre letter, plus at least two others.
- There is one word that uses every letter.

There are at least 40 words to be found.

▪ Link Words ▪

BIRD _ _ _ _ LESS

SPACE _ _ _ _ _ _ _ MAN

DRIFT _ _ _ _ CHUCK

FREE _ _ _ _ CUFFED

VIE _ _ _ LOCK

Instructions

Find a common English word to place in each gap, so that you make two new words – one when you join that word to the end of the first word, and one when you join that word to the start of the second word.

• For example, 'birth _ _ _ break' could be solved using 'day', making birthday and daybreak.

Your solving time: _____

▪ Codeword ▪

A		25	26	14	3	16	5	1		14	9	5	9	**N**
B	20		11		5		13		17		4		20	**O**
C	22	5	18	20	14 **A**	9	5		5	4	14	10	25	**P**
D	11		23		1 **R**		18	20		5		9		**Q**
E	26	20	9	9	11		7	20	9	7	5	2		**R**
F	10				26		9		14		8		2	**S**
G	9	5	20	9	11	3		22	1	5	5	8	5	**T**
H	21		4		16		14		5				6	**U**
I		22	14	19	10	3	16		17	11	15	10	5	**V**
J	17		20		18		26			5		10	3	**W**
K	5	24	7	1	20		10	16	3	10	7	5	2	**X**
L	5		10		26 **L**		5		7		20		9	**Y**
M	23	10	18	23		12	1	5	9	7	26	5		**Z**

1	2	3	4	5	6	7	8	9	10	11	12	13
14	15	16	17	18	19	20	21	22	23	24	25	26

Instructions

Solve this coded crossword in which every letter has been replaced by a number, indicated by the small digits in the top-left corner of each square.

- Work out which number represents each letter of the alphabet, and use this information to complete the grid.
- Keep track of the code by using the boxes beneath the puzzle, and the used letters with the letters outside the grid.

Your solving time: _____

▪ Spiral Crossword ▪

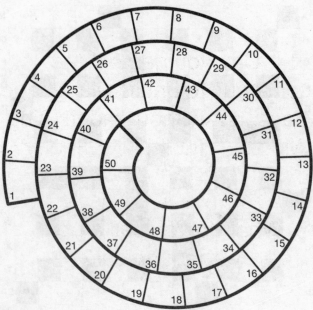

Inward

1-5   Adhesive mixture
6-10   Andean transport animal
11-13   Bottle top
14-18   Tag
19-24   Cream-filled cake
25-32   Capturing
33-35   Bad hair discovery
36-41   Walk like a baby
42-46   Hand-to-forearm joint
47-50   'Bother!'

Outward

50-46   Begin
45-43   Polite form of address
42-39   Fuse
38-32   Completing the 'i's?
31-29   Sharp bite
28-26   Golfing average
25-21   Courtroom event
20-16   Paparazzi target
15-10   Llama relative
9-4   Large, wooden hammer
3-1   Gullible fool

Instructions

Solve the clues and write the answers in the given direction.

      Your solving time: _____

▪ Word Riddles ▪

Can you name three
consecutive English-language
days, but without mentioning
Monday, Tuesday or Friday?

What do you call a bear
without an ear?

Instructions
Can you solve both of the riddles above?

- The riddles work by using word plays, e.g. by deliberately
using a different meaning of a word to that expected.

▪ Arrow Word ▪

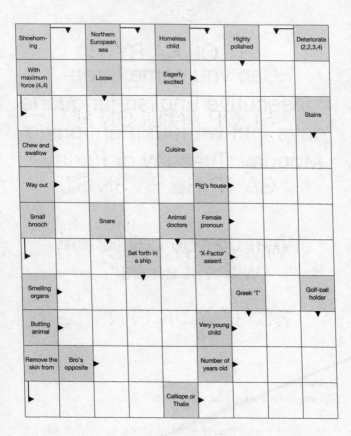

Instructions

Solve this crossword in which all of the clues are given within the grid.

• Each arrow points to where the answer should be written.

Your solving time: _____

▪ Deleted Pairs ▪

GT OL KA RY TO

SL OP AN DI ON NY

GA TR HE EA SN ST

WM AO ST HC OI WN

BC HE AI JN EI NS TG

Instructions

Delete one letter from each pair in order to reveal a set of five capital cities.

- For example, given DC RO LG you could cross out the C, R and L to leave DOG: D̶C̶ R̶O̶ L̶G.

■ Every Second Letter ■

_O_A_T

_E_T_O_E_

_H_P_N

_C_U_E_T

_I_A_D_

Instructions

Can you identify all five of these composers?

• Every other letter has been removed from each word, so 'example' could have been written as either E_A_P_E or as _X_M_L_.

Your solving time: _____

▪ Word Square ▪

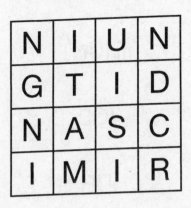

N	I	U	N
G	T	I	D
N	A	S	C
I	M	I	R

_____

_____

_____

_____

_____

_____

Instructions

How many words can you find in the word square above?

- Spell each word by starting on any letter and then moving left/right/up/down to adjacent letters, without revisiting any square within a word.
- There is one word that uses every letter.

There are at least 20 words to be found.

Your solving time: _____

▪ First and Last ▪

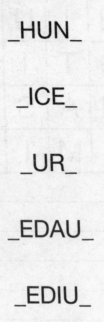

HUN

ICE

_UR_

EDAU

EDIU

Instructions

The same letter has been removed from the start and end of each word above, with a different letter for each word.

- Identify the missing letter for each line, and restore the original words.

Your solving time: _____

■ A-Z Crossword ■

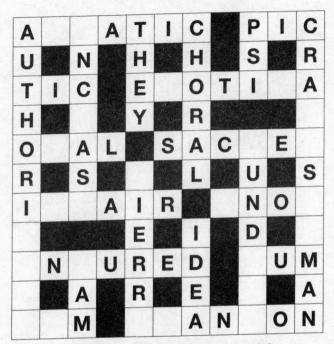

A B C D E F G H I J K L M
N O P Q R S T U V W X Y Z

Instructions

Complete this crossword grid so that each horizontal and vertical run of white squares spells a word.

- Each letter from A to Z is missing exactly once from the grid.
- Use the letters beneath the grid to keep track of which letters are remaining to be placed.

Your solving time: _____

▪ Starting Sequences ▪

O T T F F S S

GW JA TJ JM JM JA

TMN TLTWATW THAHB PC TVOTDT TSC

Instructions

Can you identify each of the sequences above, and then say what letter, or set of letters, should come next?

- The first letters of words or names are given.
- Each sequence is based on either general knowledge or on word meanings. For example, M T W T F S would be followed by Sunday since these are the days of the week: Monday, Tuesday, Wednesday, Thursday, Friday, Saturday, Sunday.

Your solving time: _____

▪ World Heritage Sites Word Search ▪

E	L	S	B	M	D	A	N	G	K	O	R	A	M	T
E	F	T	R	O	T	E	L	A	R	Y	M	L	A	P
S	R	A	A	R	E	N	B	R	A	A	S	B	C	E
E	A	T	S	I	C	O	L	L	U	E	G	G	Q	E
D	S	U	I	A	I	T	A	A	A	A	R	A	U	C
A	E	E	L	C						S	A	M	A	I
L	R	O	I	C						T	N	O	R	N
G	I	F	A	I						E	D	U	I	E
R	S	L	Y	R						R	C	N	E	V
E	L	I	K	O						I	A	T	I	F
V	A	B	A	T	A	E	T	A	S	S	N	W	S	O
E	N	E	K	S	T	Y	R	W	U	L	Y	U	L	Y
E	D	R	A	I	H	T	Y	I	B	A	O	Y	A	T
Y	A	T	D	H	E	E	N	O	A	N	N	I	N	I
Y	R	Y	U	P	S	I	E	N	A	D	E	M	D	C

ABU SIMBEL	KAKADU
ANGKOR	LAKE MALAWI
BRASILIA	MACQUARIE ISLAND
CITY OF BATH	MOUNT WUYI
CITY OF VENICE	PALMYRA
EASTER ISLAND	PETRA
EVERGLADES	SIENA
FRASER ISLAND	STATUE OF LIBERTY
GRAND CANYON	TAJ MAHAL
HISTORIC CAIRO	YELLOWSTONE

Instructions

Complete the grid by finding all of the listed entries.

Your solving time: _____

▪ Mixed Pairs ▪

SGIARMFUONNKEL

HOAALTELS

SCHONENRY

LMCECANRTNNOENY

ITKINEA

Instructions

Five musical duos are given, each of which consists of two parts separated by 'and'. The letters from the two parts have then been mixed together, although without changing the order of the letters within either part.

• For example, 'alive and kicking' could be written as **ALIKIVCKIENG**, or as **KAILCKIVINEG**.

Your solving time: _____

▪ Letter Soup ▪

Instructions

Can you rearrange these letters to reveal five trees?

- Each letter is used in exactly one of the five answers, and each answer is a single word.

▪ Initial Letters ▪

M-D by HM

JE by CB

IKWTCBS by MA

MD by VW

TGG by FSF

Instructions

Can you identify all of these classic novels, and their
associated authors?

• Only the initial letters of each novel and author are given.

▪ Word Pyramid ▪

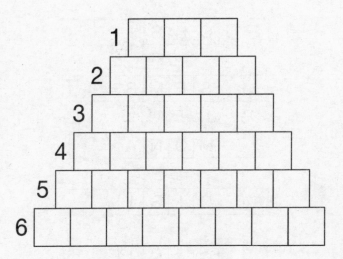

1 Doggy delivery?
2 Hope for the best
3 Mist
4 Settles a debt
5 Actors
6 In small numbers

Instructions
Solve each clue and write the answer into the corresponding row of the pyramid.

- Each row of the pyramid contains the same set of letters as the row above it, plus one extra. The letters may be in a different order, however.

▪ Zigzag ▪

Instructions

Write a letter in each grey box so that every line contains an eight-letter word.

- Each pair of grey boxes is linked to another pair of grey boxes. Each linked pair contains the same two letters, in the same relative positions.

Your solving time: _____

▪ Fit Word ▪

3 Letters
Art
Ask
Aye
Bus
Cam
Chi
Cur
Dip
Due
Egg
Hem
Hog
Kit

Lei
Lid
Moa
Own
Peg
Sat
Tut

4 Letters
Ibis
Iron
Menu
Oboe

5 Letters
Auras
Email
Evade
Guilt
Icing
Needs
Scoop
Tense
Tough
Urges

6 Letters
Manage

Modest
Stacks
Wealth

7 Letters
Bearing
Burrito
Chorizo
Shelter

Instructions

Enter each of the listed words into the grid, one letter per square. Each word should read either across or down.

Your solving time: _____

▪ Word Chains ▪

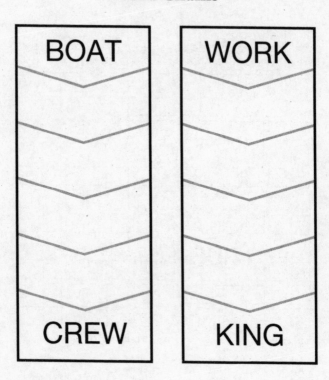

Instructions

Complete each of these two word chains by writing a four-letter word into each gap. Once complete, the top word of each chain should link to the bottom word in five steps.

• Each word must use the same letters in the same order as the word above, but with just one letter changed.

Your solving time: _____

▪ Anagrams ▪

CONTAINS AWE

BRAIN TITLE SEEN

DO ASTONISH ME

I RUE A CRIME

EVADE A LOCAL

Instructions

Each of the above is an anagram of a famous historical scientist. Can you unscramble each set of letters?

Your solving time: _____

■ Encrypted Quote ■

"Iye mkxxyd ocmkzo dro boczyxcslsvsdi yp dywybbyg li ofknsxq sd dynki."

– Klbkrkw Vsxmyvx

Instructions

The text above contains an encrypted historical quote.

- Each letter in the text has been shifted by a constant amount, so for example if the shift was up by two places then A would have been changed to C, and B to D, and C to E, and so on through until X to Z, and Y to A, and Z to B.

Your solving time: _____

▪ Crossword ▪

Across

1 *Carmen*, eg (5)
4 Beaded counting tool (6)
10 Relating to a bishop (9)
11 Grammar article (3)
12 Long-necked waterbird (5)
13 Geronimo descendant (6)
14 Confining (11)
18 Common type of acid (6)
20 What one? (5)
23 Binary digit (3)
24 Not with any serious value (9)
25 Revolve (6)
26 Feeling of dread (5)

Down

2 Self-respect (5)
3 Most affluent (7)
5 Corkwood (5)
6 Grasp; understand (5,2)
7 Search (4)
8 Horse's whinny (5)
9 Completely on-message official? (11)
15 Famous and admired (7)
16 Maternity-ward baby (7)
17 Elected (5)
19 Reinstall (5)
21 Desktop graphics (5)
22 Belonging to the reader (4)

Instructions

Solve each clue and write the answer into the grid, one letter per square. Write either across or down as indicated.

Your solving time: _____

▪ Vowelless ▪

L TT C

LK

KL

SW TP TT

NN

Instructions

All of the vowels have been removed from the vegetables above. Can you restore them to reveal the original words?

• Any existing spaces have been removed, and then some random spaces have been added to make it a little trickier.

Your solving time: _____

▪ Word Circle ▪

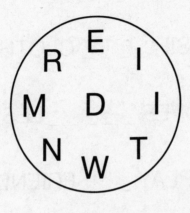

_____

_____

_____

_____

_____

Instructions

How many words can you find in the word circle above?

- Every word must use the centre letter, plus at least two others.
- There is one word that uses every letter.

There are at least 50 words to be found.

▪ Link Words ▪

SIR _ _ _ _ CLOTH

OVER _ _ _ _ _ LESS

PLAY _ _ _ FRIEND

SIGN _ _ _ _ AGE

CORN _ _ _ _ _ WINNER

Instructions

Find a common English word to place in each gap, so that you make two new words – one when you join that word to the end of the first word, and one when you join that word to the start of the second word.

• For example, 'birth _ _ _ break' could be solved using 'day', making birthday and daybreak.

Your solving time: _____

▪ Codeword ▪

A		4		11		7 P		14		4		N
B	25	11	1	17	24		8	3	12	20	8	22	O
C	2		11		3		26		17		25		17	P
D	1 A	4	1	18	12	3	10		17	12	19	5	22 E	Q
E	17		26		11		22		12				3	R
F	17	12	21	3		15		23	21	16	12	3	10	S
G	21		3		19	1	16	22	3		4		19	T
H	2	22	12	10	5	19		19		11	1	25	5	U
I	12			12		6		4		10		2	V
J	3	12	22	11	22		22	13	21	19	12	11	1	W
K	10		13		9		14		3		3		24	X
L		14	1	25	22	25	19		19	26	22	25	25	Y
M			4		25		25		5		25		Z

1	2	3	4	5	6	7	8	9	10	11	12	13
14	15	16	17	18	19	20	21	22	23	24	25	26

Instructions

Solve this coded crossword in which every letter has been replaced by a number, indicated by the small digits in the top-left corner of each square.

- Work out which number represents each letter of the alphabet, and use this information to complete the grid.
- Keep track of the code by using the boxes beneath the puzzle, and the used letters with the letters outside the grid.

Your solving time: _____

▪ Spiral Crossword ▪

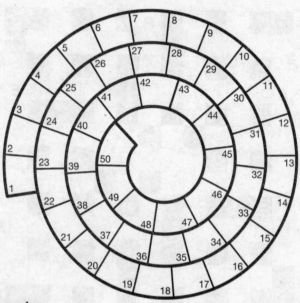

Inward

1-6   Dining furniture
7-12 In the air
13-19 Widespread
20-22 Slack
23-28 Is
29-33 Strike together, as teeth
34-39 Hard-shelled sea animal
40-46 Ten to the ninth power
47-50 Hospital room

Outward

50-46 Illustrated
45-43 Vegetable or palm, eg
42-38 Defamatory publication
37-32 Facts
31-27 Feeling of dread
26-24 Lowest clock numeral
23-19 Speak highly of
18-16 Quick rest
15-13 Detract from
12-9 Wild animal's home
8-4   Artist's stand
3-1   Cricketing essential

Instructions

Solve the clues and write the answers in the given direction.

Your solving time: _____

■ Word Riddles ■

According to the plays, which Shakespearian character killed the most birds?

There is something so fragile that just saying its name will break it. What is it?

Instructions

Can you solve both of the riddles above?

- The riddles work by using word plays, e.g. by deliberately using a different meaning of a word to that expected.

▪ Arrow Word ▪

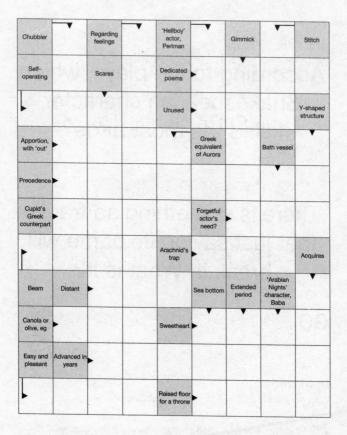

Instructions

Solve this crossword in which all of the clues are given within the grid.

• Each arrow points to where the answer should be written.

Your solving time: _____

▪ Deleted Pairs ▪

SJ UT NR LK

YO PA PC IH TN

CF RE RA RD TY

HC AO NO RO EK

GC AO TO AD NM EA SR SA NY

Instructions

Delete one letter from each pair in order to reveal a set of five types of boat.

- For example, given DC RO LG you could cross out the C, R and L to leave DOG: D~~C~~ ~~R~~O ~~L~~G.

Your solving time: _____   117

▪ Every Second Letter ▪

_O_K

_A_A_I

_H_C_E_

_U_T_N

_E_I_O_

Instructions

Can you identify all five of these meats?

- Every other letter has been removed from each word, so 'example' could have been written as either E_A_P_E or as _X_M_L_.

Your solving time: _____

■ Word Square ■

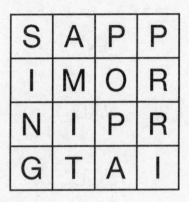

_____

_____

_____

_____

_____

_____

Instructions

How many words can you find in the word square above?

- Spell each word by starting on any letter and then moving left/right/up/down to adjacent letters, without revisiting any square within a word.
- There is one word that uses every letter.

There are at least 30 words to be found.

Your solving time: _____   119

▪ First and Last ▪

INI

VAD

ECU

LUIN

_W_

Instructions

The same letter has been removed from the start and end of each word above, with a different letter for each word.

• Identify the missing letter for each line, and restore the original words.

Your solving time: _____

▪ A-Z Crossword ▪

A B C D E F G H I J K L M
N O P Q R S T U V W X Y Z

Instructions

Complete this crossword grid so that each horizontal and vertical run of white squares spells a word.

- Each letter from A to Z is missing exactly once from the grid.
- Use the letters beneath the grid to keep track of which letters are remaining to be placed.

▪ Starting Sequences ▪

HTQFSS

ATGCLVLSSCA

DD PP LL LD MM SS GL

Instructions

Can you identify each of the sequences above, and then say what letter, or set of letters, should come next?

- The first letters of words or names are given.
- Each sequence is based on either general knowledge or on word meanings. For example, M T W T F S would be followed by Sunday since these are the days of the week: Monday, Tuesday, Wednesday, Thursday, Friday, Saturday, Sunday.

Your solving time: _____

▪ Shakespearean Tragedy Word Search ▪

L	I	R	T	I	A	O	T	H	E	L	L	O	J	A
S	G	A	A	L	M	E	R	C	U	T	I	O	N	I
S	F	U	J	S	S	U	I	N	O	L	O	P	M	A
K	F	O	B	R	E	R	H	A	I	T	R	O	P	U
I	U	H	C	O	O	A	C	O	S	R	P	R	T	C
N	D	L	T	M					E	G	D	I	L	
G	C	Y	E	E					A	E	O	S	E	
L	A	O	N	E					S	T	U	A	O	
E	M	A	R	O					I	I	I	N	P	
A	I	O	I	O					D	L	H	O	A	
R	A	R	I	L	R	N	M	M	U	O	A	U	H	T
I	G	R	E	E	E	O	A	A	Y	M	O	I	J	R
L	O	U	G	S	N	H	L	E	L	D	O	B	P	A
C	R	A	O	A	N	C	P	E	M	I	A	E	E	U
C	S	U	T	U	R	B	T	O	T	E	I	L	U	J

ANTONY	GERTRUDE	MACDUFF
BRUTUS	HAMLET	MERCUTIO
CASSIO	HORATIO	OPHELIA
CICERO	IAGO	OTHELLO
CLAUDIUS	JULIET	POLONIUS
CLEOPATRA	JULIUS CAESAR	PORTIA
CORIOLANUS	KING LEAR	ROMEO
DESDEMONA	LADY MACBETH	

Instructions

Find all these entries in the grid, in any direction. The middle of the grid is missing and must be restored.

▪ Mixed Pairs ▪

ABBEYOONVED

BSWAITITCH

HIDGRHY

LLIEVAREN

NAGOAWIN

Instructions

Five common phrases are given, each of which consists of two parts separated by 'and'. The letters from the two parts have then been mixed together, although without changing the order of the letters within either part.

- For example, 'alive and kicking' could be written as **ALIKIVCKIENG**, or as **KAILCKIVINEG**.

Your solving time: _____

▪ Letter Soup ▪

Instructions

Can you rearrange these letters to reveal five items of furniture?

- Each letter is used in exactly one of the five answers, and each answer is a single word.

▪ **Initial Letters** ▪

TR by EAP

I by RK

IWLAAC by WW

TRNT by RF

DNGGITGN by DT

Instructions

Can you identify all of these famous poems titles, and their associated poets?

• Only the initial letters of each title and poet are given.

Your solving time: _____

▪ Word Pyramid ▪

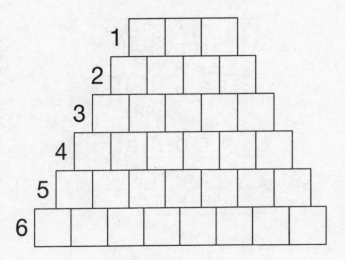

1 Free
2 Avian
3 Nuptial partner
4 Rubble
5 Paper organizers
6 Strong spirits

Instructions

Solve each clue and write the answer into the corresponding row of the pyramid.

- Each row of the pyramid contains the same set of letters as the row above it, plus one extra. The letters may be in a different order, however.

Your solving time: _____

127

▪ Zigzag ▪

| T | R | E | A | S | U | | |

| | | F | O | R | M | | |

| | | T | O | R | N | | |

| | | E | P | I | E | | |

| | | L | I | B | A | | |

| | | C | L | O | N | | |

| | | C | A | P | I | S | M |

Instructions

Write a letter in each grey box so that every line contains an eight-letter word.

- Each pair of grey boxes is linked to another pair of grey boxes. Each linked pair contains the same two letters, in the same relative positions.

Your solving time: _____

▪ Fit Word ▪

3 Letters
Awe
Bow
Cad
Did
Gin
Guy
Hew
Hid
Hue
Lob
Low
Mic
Mow

Nab
Net
Opt
Red
Rim
Soy
Tag
Who
Win
Wow

4 Letters
Dewy
Eras

Mire
Mope
Stew
Unit

5 Letters
Apron
Colon
Doyen
Inept
Paged
Spoof

6 Letters
Adhere
Fiesta
Hordes
Second

7 Letters
Debated
Limited

Instructions

Enter each of the listed words into the grid, one letter per square. Each word should read either across or down.

Your solving time: _____

▪ Word Chains ▪

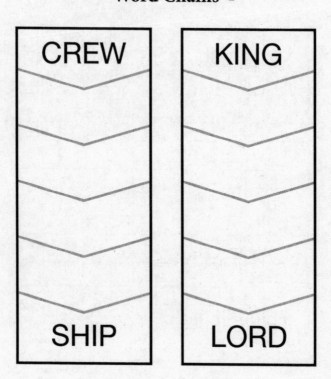

Instructions

Complete each of these two word chains by writing a four-letter word into each gap. Once complete, the top word of each chain should link to the bottom word in five steps.

- Each word must use the same letters in the same order as the word above, but with just one letter changed.

Your solving time: _____

▪ Anagrams ▪

DUAL ARC

TWITS OR EVIL

FINE TEN RANKS

ITEM NOT WELL

THUGGISH WHITENER

Instructions

Each of the above is an anagram of the title of a classic work of literature. Can you unscramble each set of letters?

▪ **Encrypted Quote** ▪

"Gh ftg, yhk tgr vhglbwxktuex
ixkbhw, vtg pxtk hgx ytvx
mh abflxey tgw tghmaxk
mh max fnembmnwx,
pbmahnm ybgteer zxmmbgz
uxpbewxkxw tl mh pabva ftr
ux max mknx."

– Gtmatgbxe Atpmahkgx

Instructions
The text above contains an encrypted historical quote.

- Each letter in the text has been shifted by a constant
  amount, so for example if the shift was up by two places
  then A would have been changed to C, and B to D, and C to
  E, and so on through until X to Z, and Y to A, and Z to B.

Your solving time: _____

▪ Crossword ▪

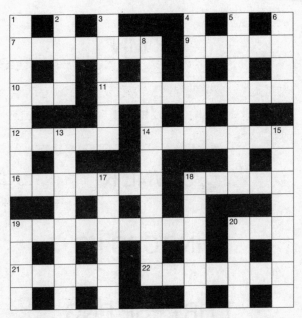

Across
- **7** Pull out (7)
- **9** Kept an engine running (5)
- **10** 'Harrumph!' (3)
- **11** Skilled, elder politician (9)
- **12** Bronze medal position (5)
- **14** Thwarts (7)
- **16** Letter; dispatch (7)
- **18** Hazardous (5)
- **19** No longer worried (9)
- **20** Lass (3)
- **21** Chickpea or lentil (5)
- **22** Periods of ten years (7)

Down
- **1** Word for word (8)
- **2** Hankering (4)
- **3** Elapsed (6)
- **4** Animated (6)
- **5** International games (8)
- **6** Japanese pasta strips (4)
- **8** Moved from one place to another (11)
- **13** Sets up (8)
- **15** Small telescope (8)
- **17** Reply (6)
- **18** Deplete (6)
- **19** Fibrous (4)
- **20** Supreme beings (4)

Instructions

Solve each clue and write the answer into the grid, one letter per square. Write either across or down as indicated.

Your solving time: _____

■ Vowelless ■

CR MN

R PH S

S WNL K

THN TCRC KR

T HRT FSP RNG

Instructions

All of the vowels have been removed from the famous ballets above. Can you restore them to reveal the original words?

• Any existing spaces have been removed, and then some random spaces have been added to make it a little trickier.

Your solving time: _____

▪ Word Circle ▪

_____

_____

_____

_____

_____

_____

Instructions

How many words can you find in the word circle above?

- Every word must use the centre letter, plus at least two others.
- There is one word that uses every letter.

There are at least 40 words to be found.

▪ Link Words ▪

WAR _ _ _ _ WAY

OVER _ _ _ _ TICK

GANG _ _ _ _ _ TON

TIME _ _ _ _ _ TOP

MINI _ _ _ GUARD

Instructions

Find a common English word to place in each gap, so that you make two new words – one when you join that word to the end of the first word, and one when you join that word to the start of the second word.

• For example, 'birth _ _ _ break' could be solved using 'day', making birthday and daybreak.

Your solving time: _____

▪ Codeword ▪

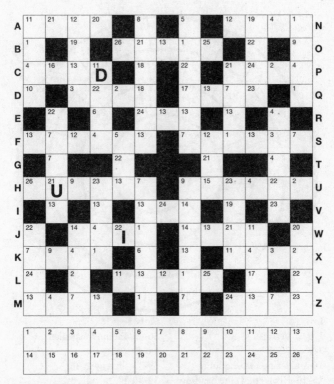

Instructions

Solve this coded crossword in which every letter has been replaced by a number, indicated by the small digits in the top-left corner of each square.

- Work out which number represents each letter of the alphabet, and use this information to complete the grid.
- Keep track of the code by using the boxes beneath the puzzle, and the used letters with the letters outside the grid.

Your solving time: _____   137

▪ Spiral Crossword ▪

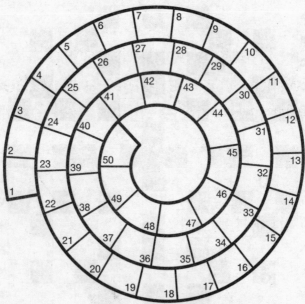

Inward

1-6 Vestiges
7-9 Fury
10-14 Serious wrongdoing
15-20 Horizontal clue heading
21-23 Stop
24-28 Mexican friend
29-33 Give up
34-36 Up until, poetically
37-41 Begin to wilt
42-46 Subway
47-50 Edible root

Outward

50-45 Eloquent speaker
44-40 Pace
39-33 Sent away for
32-30 Floral offering
29-26 Asana teacher
25-19 Insanity
18-15 Black-and-white, toothed whale
14-11 Muslim ruler
10-5 Cherry red
4-1 Wagon

Instructions

Solve the clues and write the answers in the given direction.

Your solving time: _____

▪ Word Riddles ▪

There is something from which you can take away the whole, and yet still have some left. What is it?

In what way is the letter 'a' just like noon?

Instructions

Can you solve both of the riddles above?

- The riddles work by using word plays, e.g. by deliberately using a different meaning of a word to that expected.

▪ Arrow Word ▪

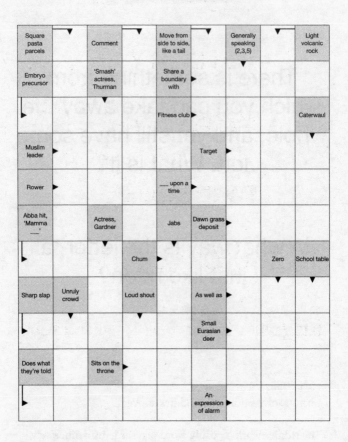

Instructions

Solve this crossword in which all of the clues are given within the grid.

• Each arrow points to where the answer should be written.

Your solving time: _____

▪ Starting Sequences ▪

F M A M J J A

R D J L B A S A B S

JW PC MS DT CE PM SM CB

Instructions

Can you identify each of the sequences above, and then say what letter, or set of letters, should come next?

The first letters of words or names are given.
Each sequence is based on either general knowledge or on word meanings. For example, M T W T F S would be followed by Sunday since these are the days of the week: Monday, Tuesday, Wednesday, Thursday, Friday, Saturday, Sunday.

Your solving time: _____

▪ Word Square ▪

R	P	P	A
E	H	S	S
N	E	E	N
S	I	V	E

_____

_____

_____

_____

_____

Instructions

How many words can you find in the word square above?

• Spell each word by starting on any letter and then moving left/right/up/down to adjacent letters, without revisiting any square within a word.
• There is one word that uses every letter.

There are at least 25 words to be found.

Your solving time: _____

143

▪ First and Last ▪

UPE

CACI

_AV_

ASBA

ALLO

Instructions

The same letter has been removed from the start and end of each word above, with a different letter for each word.

- Identify the missing letter for each line, and restore the original words.

Your solving time: _____

▪ A-Z Crossword ▪

A B C D E F G H I J K L M
N O P Q R S T U V W X Y

Instructions

Complete this crossword grid so that each horizo vertical run of white squares spells a word.

- Each letter from A to Z is missing exactly once grid.
- Use the letters beneath the grid to keep track letters are remaining to be placed.

Your solving time: _____

▪ Greetings Cards Word Search ▪

F	A	T	H	E	R	S	D	A	Y	I	G	T	A	G
E	H	W	H	P	N	H	M	B	S	N	P	V	P	E
S	Y	A	N	I	N	W	A	S	I	O	A	A	S	T
U	A	P	P	E	N	B	I	V	I	L	R	U	S	W
O	D	I	E	P	W	K	A	T	E	T	A	R	U	E
H	S	A	N	E					C	P	O	Y	L
W	R	N	N	T					L	Y	A	I	L
E	E	E	E	E					K	O	L	B	S
N	H	H	R	W					O	A	V	E	O
E	T	U	P	E					W	F	B	E	O
E	O	H	S	O	U	O	H	Y	I	E	K	Y	Y	N
Y	M	D	K	J	I	T	B	D	I	T	R	A	O	A
Y	A	D	H	T	R	I	B	Y	P	P	A	H	T	U
Y	N	Y	A	N	N	I	V	E	R	S	A	R	Y	N
E	T	H	A	P	P	Y	N	E	W	Y	E	A	R	A

ANNIVERSARY
BAPTISM
DIWALI
FATHER'S DAY
GET WELL SOON
HAPPY BIRTHDAY
HAPPY EASTER
HAPPY NEW YEAR
JUST BECAUSE
MOTHER'S DAY

NEW BABY
NEW HOUSE
NEW JOB
SAINT'S DAY
SORRY
THANK YOU
THINKING OF YOU
VALENTINE'S DAY
WITH LOVE
YOU'RE LEAVING

Instructions
Complete the grid by finding all of the listed entries.

▪ Mixed Pairs ▪

TRTINOBIADAGDO

BHEROZEGSONVIINAA

ABANTRIGBUUDAA

SANINETKVIITSTS

SPRAOINTCOMIPEE

Instructions

Five countries are given, each of which consists of two parts separated by 'and'. The letters from the two parts have then been mixed together, although without changing the order of the letters within either part.

• For example, 'alive and kicking' could be written as **ALIKIVCKIENG**, or as **KAILCKIVINEG**.

Your solving time: _____

▪ Letter Soup ▪

Instructions

Can you rearrange these letters to reveal five bodily organs?

- Each letter is used in exactly one of the five answers, and each answer is a single word.

▪ Initial Letters ▪

BJ by MJ

BTB by AW

TOM by A-H

NWNC by BM

AOBTD by Q

Instructions

Can you identify all of these song titles, and their associated artists?

• Only the initial letters of each title and artist is given.

Your solving time: _____

▪ Word Pyramid ▪

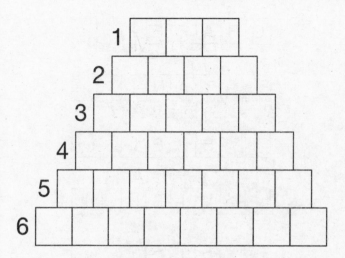

1 Wildebeest
2 Musically voiced
3 Employing
4 Sage
5 Following
6 Flightless birds

Instructions
Solve each clue and write the answer into the corresponding row of the pyramid.

- Each row of the pyramid contains the same set of letters as the row above it, plus one extra. The letters may be in a different order, however.

▪ Zigzag ▪

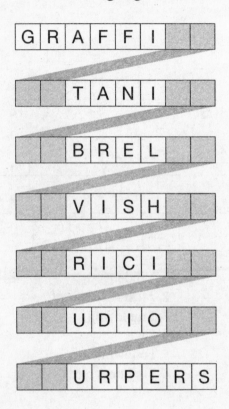

Instructions

Write a letter in each grey box so that every line contains an eight-letter word.

• Each pair of grey boxes is linked to another pair of grey boxes. Each linked pair contains the same two letters, in the same relative positions.

Your solving time: _____

▪ Fit Word ▪

3 Letters
Add
Aid
Don
Fog
Get
God
Hay
Ice
Now
Oat
Pec
Raw
Set

Sir
Tie

4 Letters
Acts
Feta
Gill
Goal
Idea
Laps
Orca
Plug
Rise
Sage

Stag
Swan
Vain
Vies

5 Letters
Ample
Ingot
Irate
Olive

6 Letters
Fender
Strips

Stupid
Theses

8 Letters
Altitude
Indulges

Instructions

Enter each of the listed words into the grid, one letter per square. Each word should read either across or down.

Your solving time: _____

▪ Word Chains ▪

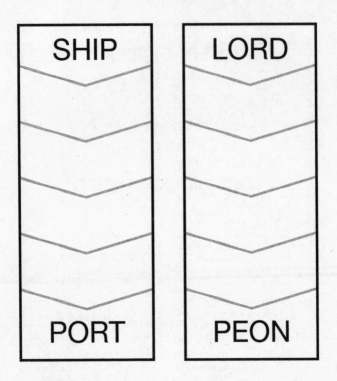

Instructions

Complete each of these two word chains by writing a four-letter word into each gap. Once complete, the top word of each chain should link to the bottom word in five steps.

• Each word must use the same letters in the same order as the word above, but with just one letter changed.

Your solving time: _____

▪ Anagrams ▪

SHY COP

CANAL AS CAB

HOG DEAR THEFT

GALE FLOODS

NOW WEIGHTED HINT

Instructions

Each of the above is an anagram of a classic movie. Can you unscramble each set of letters?

■ Encrypted Quote ■

"R fxdum jufjhb ajcqna kn qjyyh cqjw mrpwrornm."

– Lqjauxccn Kaxwcn

Instructions

The text above contains an encrypted historical quote.

• Each letter in the text has been shifted by a constant amount, so for example if the shift was up by two places then A would have been changed to C, and B to D, and C to E, and so on through until X to Z, and Y to A, and Z to B.

Your solving time: _____

▪ Crossword ▪

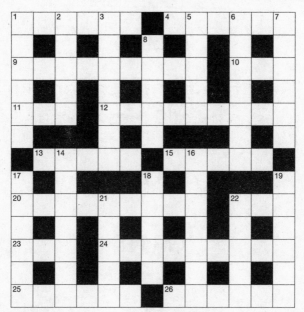

Across

1 Money earned (6)
4 Biochemical tests (6)
9 Recollects (9)
10 Fish-and-chips fish (3)
11 'Precisely as written' (3)
12 Remiss (9)
13 Strength of spirit? (5)
15 Composed (5)
20 Throat lozenge (5,4)
22 Ceylon, eg (3)
23 Letter before theta (3)
24 Gives details of (9)
25 Sandwich chain (6)
26 Climb (6)

Down

1 Flood (6)
2 Humorous (5)
3 Keepsake (7)
5 Japanese cuisine (5)
6 Extremely old (7)
7 Calm and dignified (6)
8 Rule as monarch (5)
14 Large-leaved edible plant (7)
16 Accounts (7)
17 Metal fasteners (6)
18 Light touch (5)
19 Elevated (6)
21 Monster slain by Hercules (5)
22 Furniture suitable for eating at (5)

Instructions

Solve each clue and write the answer into the grid, one letter per square. Write either across or down as indicated.

▪ **Vowelless** ▪

D MND

MR LD

J D

GR NT

PL

Instructions

All of the vowels have been removed from the types of gem above. Can you restore them to reveal the original words?

• Any existing spaces have been removed, and then some random spaces have been added to make it a little trickier.

Your solving time: _____

▪ Word Circle ▪

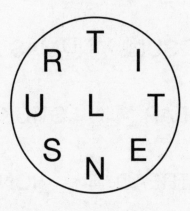

_____

_____

_____

_____

_____

Instructions

How many words can you find in the word circle above?

• Every word must use the centre letter, plus at least two others.
• There is one word that uses every letter.

There are at least 60 words to be found.

▪ Link Words ▪

BULL _ _ _ MAS

EAR _ _ _ _ STICK

TREAD _ _ _ _ ION

BACK _ _ _ JAM

READ _ _ _ _ ICE

Instructions

Find a common English word to place in each gap, so that
you make two new words – one when you join that word to
the end of the first word, and one when you join that word to
the start of the second word.

• For example, 'birth _ _ _ break' could be solved using 'day',
  making birthday and daybreak.

Your solving time: _____

▪ Codeword ▪

Instructions

Solve this coded crossword in which every letter has been replaced by a number, indicated by the small digits in the top-left corner of each square.

- Work out which number represents each letter of the alphabet, and use this information to complete the grid.
- Keep track of the code by using the boxes beneath the puzzle, and the used letters with the letters outside the grid.

Your solving time: _____

▪ Spiral Crossword ▪

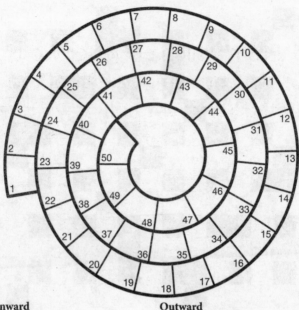

Inward

1-5   Lots
6-11 To settle comfortably
12-16 Ecstasy
17-21 Tender
22-26 Church tenets
27-32 Blending music tracks
33-35 Non-existent
36-40 TV without pictures?
41-45 100 aurar, in Iceland
46-50 Written reminder notes

Outward

50-47 A few
46-42 Large country house
41-39 Large, ornamental carp
38-32 Cherished
31-29 Veto
28-25 Muslim leader
24-22 Christian creator of all
21-19 Sports arbiter
18-13 Prehistoric remains
12-9 Judo ranking item
8-4   Touch or taste
3-1   Edge

Instructions

Solve the clues and write the answers in the given direction.

Your solving time: _____

▪ Word Riddles ▪

From which six letter word can you remove half of the letters and yet only have one left?

What is it that always ends up with just a nose, whenever it loses an eye?

Instructions
Can you solve both of the riddles above?

• The riddles work by using word plays, e.g. by deliberately using a different meaning of a word to that expected.

▪ Arrow Word ▪

'Much ___ About Nothing'	▼	Get this clue wrong, eg	▼	Vehicle for transporting goods	▼	Large, burning torch		Buffoons
Complete lack of success (4,4) ►		▼						
►				Dark-brown pigment		Michael Jackson hit		Greek letter following pi
Given birth to	Snapshot		Hasty			▼		▼
Reckoned	▼	Jabber		Clobber ►				
►		▼					Sends a parcel	
Lotus or Seat, eg ►				Roulette bet, perhaps		Adhesive	▼	Trial
Fanatical	Initiated, as in a legal action ►				▼			▼
►				Stretch out, maybe ►				
Plant's starting point	Fronted ►			Backup electricity source (inits)				
►			Garment worn on the top half of your body					

Instructions

Solve this crossword in which all of the clues are given within the grid.

• Each arrow points to where the answer should be written.

Your solving time: _____

■ Deleted Pairs ■

GR EA DN

SB LO UA TC KS

VN OE RL TT HA

DB AR LN UT BI CY

AC MA SA PZ IO IA NT

Instructions

Delete one letter from each pair in order to reveal a set of five seas.

• For example, given DC RO LG you could cross out the C, R and L to leave DOG: D̶C̶ R̶O̶ L̶G̶.

▪ Solutions ▪

Page 7

1 AMP
2 PALM
3 MAPLE
4 SAMPLE
5 IMPALES
6 MISPLACE

Page 8

P A C I F I S T
S T A G N A T E
T E M P O R A L
A L F A L F A S
A S S A S S I N
I N N U E N D O
D O C U M E N T

Page 9

T · RAG · SATANIC
O · E · O · U · O · I · O
TAP · OHM · FILLS
E · · · · · · FUR
MARKER · L · KITE
· L · E · A · O · · R
PING · VIA · FOUR
· K · · A · T · I · N
MEGA · G · STRIKE
· · · · SUE · · · · · B
BATHS · OWE · PRO
E · I · E · L · L · A · N
ENCODED · MAW · Y

Page 10

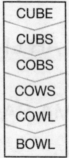

CUBE
CUBS
COBS
COWS
COWL
BOWL

DOWN
TOWN
TORN
TERN
TERM
TEAM

Page 11

- UNITED KINGDOM
- AUSTRALIA
- BARBADOS
- MONGOLIA
- AFGHANISTAN

Page 12

The letters have been shifted forward 4 places:

"If your actions inspire others to dream more, to learn more, do more and become more, you are a leader."

– John Quincy Adams

▪ Solutions ▪

Page 13

D	E	P	T	H	S		A	B	S	E	I	L
E		L		O			U		A		E	
E	M	U		C	A	T	A	M	A	R	A	N
P		N		K		H		P		N		S
L	A	D	S		D	E	D	I	C	A	T	E
Y		E		I		M		N		U		S
		R	E	S	P	E	C	T	E	D		
O		E		O		P		O		I		M
W	O	R	K	L	O	A	D		S	E	G	A
N				A		R		S		N		R
I	D	E	N	T	I	K	I	T		C	O	O
N		Y		E				I		E		O
G	R	E	A	S	Y		P	R	I	S	O	N

Page 15

Words include: abolish, **abolished**, ash, ashed, bah, bahs, bash, bashed, behold, beholds, bosh, dash, dish, had, hail, hailed, hails, hale, haled, hales, halo, haloed, halos, has, head, heads, heal, heals, held, hid, hide, hides, hie, hied, hies, his, hob, hobs, hod, hods, hoe, hoed, hoes, hold, holds, hole, holed, holes, hose, hosed, lash, lashed, leash, ohs, sahib, shad, shade, shale, she, shed, shied, shield, shoal, shoaled, shod, shoe.

Page 17

	A		L		O		A		L		Z
A	L	P	A	C	A		Q	U	I	T	E
	O		I		F	L	U		R		A
D	R	E	A	R	Y		A	V	A	I	L
O		N			P		I		F		
E	X	O	T	I	C		A	V	E	R	S
S		U		L	O	P		Y			S
	K	R	O	N	A		A	S	L	E	E
O		N		Y		E		E			E
B	I	T	E	R		J	I	G	S	A	W
U		W		A	R	K		F			E
S	N	I	F	F		I	N	F	A	M	Y
H		N		T		N		Y			I

Page 14

- AMAZON
- RIO GRANDE
- THAMES
- ORINOCO
- GANGES

Page 16

- TENS: FLATTENS and TENSION
- LIFE: NIGHTLIFE and LIFEBOAT
- TRAP: BOOTSTRAP and TRAPPINGS
- MOON: HONEYMOON and MOONBEAM
- DRIFT: SNOWDRIFT and DRIFTWOOD

Page 18

Inward 1 WANGLES;
8 SEVEN; **13** ANIMA;
18 SLAB; **22** YAW; **25** ETA;
28 GRABBING; **36** NITS;
40 OPPOSED; **47** ACED

Outward 50 DECADE; **44** SOP;
41 POSTING; **34** NIB; **31** BAR;
28 GATEWAY; **21** BALSAM;
15 INANE; **10** VESSEL;
4 GNAW

▪ Solutions ▪

Page 19
- The word 'incorrectly'
- An envelope

Page 20

	P	G		D		R	
	U	R		I	D	O	L
I	N	F	O		N	I	B
	J	O	W	L		S	O	T
	A	P	T		O	T	T	O
	B	H			U	S	E
V	I	V		W	A	R	
		A		A		B	A	R
S	A	L	A	D		I	R	E
	N		L	E	A	N	E	D
T	Y	P	E	D		G	A	S

Page 21
- OWL
- HAWK
- EAGLE
- CANARY
- PENGUIN

Page 22
- PEGASUS
- URSA MINOR
- SAGITTARIUS
- AQUARIUS
- CASSIOPEIA

Page 23
Words include: arid, arider, ate, die, ear, eat, eater, eats, eider, eiders, end, ester, eta, irate, near, neat, neater, nest, rat, rate, rats, red, rid, ride, rider, riders, sea, sear, seat, secret, secretaries, secrets, send, sender, senders, star, sun, sunder, sunders, tar, terse, under, **undersecretaries**, undies, use

Page 24
- A: AGENDA
- C: CAUSTIC
- S: STUDIOS
- L: LOCAL
- M: MAIM

▪ Solutions ▪

Page 25

Page 26

- U – planets outwards from the sun: Mercury, Venus, Earth, Mars, Jupiter, Saturn, Uranus
- S – ordinals: first, second, third, fourth, fifth, sixth, seventh
- TLJ – episodes 1 to 8 *Star Wars* film subtitles: *The Phantom Menace; Attack of the Clones; Revenge of the Sith; A New Hope; The Empire Strikes Back; Return of the Jedi; The Force Awakens; The Last Jedi*

Page 27

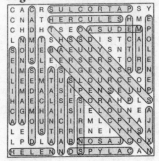

Page 28

- DAZED and CONFUSED
- THELMA and LOUISE
- BONNIE and CLYDE
- ANTONY and CLEOPATRA
- BUTCH CASSIDY and THE SUNDANCE KID

Page 29

- BLUE
- GREEN
- ORANGE
- RED
- YELLOW

Page 30

- *A Clockwork Orange* by Stanley Kubrick
- *Citizen Kane* by Orson Welles
- *Some Like It Hot* by Billy Wilder
- *Pulp Fiction* by Quentin Tarantino
- *Lost In Translation* by Sofia Coppola

▪ Solutions ▪

Page 31
1 MAP
2 RAMP
3 CRAMP
4 CAMPER
5 SCAMPER
6 COMPARES

Page 32

GLUMMEST
STATUTES
ESTRANGE
GENEROUS
USEFULLY
LYNCHPIN
INSTALLS

Page 33

```
T  TEN  H  B   M   O
HER  OVARY   EON
R  I   R  L  E   M  L
UNCOMMON   GOBY
S  K   A   N   E
TRY  ADS  BALL
   A  P   O   W  O
   CALF  WIG  EWE
   K  U   O   D  S
ASKS  BENEFITS
L  E  P  M  N   B  A
SIP  SQUAD  LAY
O  T   I  S   SEE  S
```

Page 34

BACK
HACK
HOCK
HONK
HONE
HOME

TEAM
TEAL
TELL
TALL
GALL
GALA

Page 35
- FERRARI
- PORSCHE
- BUGATTI
- ASTON MARTIN
- LAMBORGHINI

Page 36
The letters have been shifted forward 13 places.

"In matters of style, swim with the current; in matters of principle, stand like a rock."

– Thomas Jefferson

▪ Solutions ▪

Page 37

T	E	M	P	O		O	F	F	E	N	D	S
X		R		D		O		L		E		
T	I	R	A	M	I	S	U		F	A	C	E
T		Y		S		R		I		I		
A	S	S	E	T	S		T	U	N	E	D	
R		R		E		H		E				
P	I	E	S		R	Y	E		P	O	D	S
N				T		S		R				
M	O	C	H	A		T	R	O	J	A	N	
A		O		T		A		T		D		
S	T	A	Y		I	N	T	H	E	A	I	R
E		P		O		E		S		S		E
I	S	S	U	I	N	G		S	T	O	U	T

Page 39 (continued)

caste, caster, cat, cater, caters, cats, chair, chairs, chaise, char, chariest, **charities**, chars, chart, charts, chase, chaser, chaste, chaster, chat, chats, cheat, cheats, chest, chi, cite, cites, cities, crash, crate, crates, crest, cries, each, etch, ethic, ethics, ice, ices, icier, iciest, itch, itches, itchier, race, races, raciest, reach, react, reacts, recast, rice, rices, rich, riches, richest, sac, sachet, scar, scare, search, sect, sic, starch, teach, techs, thrice, trace, traces, trice

Page 41

S		C		P		R		C		F
P	I	Z	Z	A	S		O	T	H	E	R	S
X		A		Y		C		E		A
S	T	A	R		C	R	O	S	S	I	N	G
E		C		H		C		T		K
N	E	E	D	L	E	P	O	I	N	T
		N		U				U		E
	P	R	O	S	E	C	U	T	I	N	G
	T		A		M		A			J
Q	U	I	T	T	I	N	G		B	O	O	T
B		L		I		I		O		Y
R	E	M	O	V	E		L	A	W	Y	E	R
S		N		S		Y		S		D

Page 38

- GUITAR
- EUPHONIUM
- PIANO
- MOUTH ORGAN
- UKULELE

Page 39

Words include: ace, aces, ache, aches, acre, acres, act, acts, arc, arch, arches, archest, arcs, car, care, cares, caret, carets, caries, cars, cart, carts, case, cash, cashier, cast,

Page 40

- WARD: EASTWARD and WARDROBE
- WALK: CATWALK and WALKOUT
- PIECE: MOUTHPIECE and PIECEWORK
- PRICK: PINPRICK and PRICKLED
- WHERE: EVERYWHERE and WHEREUPON

Page 42

Inward 1 GARDEN;
7 ECSTASY; **14** ADD;
17 IMPALES; **24** REV;
27 DEER; **31** GRUFF; **36** FATS;
40 DELL; **44** IFS; **47** REEL

Outward 50 LEERS;
45 FILLED; **39** STAFF; **34** FUR;
31 GREED; **26** VERSE; **21** LAP;
18 MIDDAY; **12** SAT; **9** SCENE;
4 DRAG

▪ Solutions ▪

Page 43
- A teapot (since it is full of 'T'/tea)
- In a dictionary

Page 44

	E		C		P		A	
	X		E		R	A	G	E
S	P	E	L	L	I	N	G	
	I	L	L		M	I	L	K
	R	I	O			M	O	E
F	E	Z		D		A	M	Y
	A	P	E	S		E		
	B	I	N		E	R	E	
F	L	E	X		F	L	A	P
	T	I	M		A	T	E	
A	C	H	E		K	N	E	E

Page 45
- COD
- HAKE
- SHARK
- HADDOCK
- MACKEREL

Page 46
- ENGLISH
- SPANISH
- MANDARIN
- PORTUGUESE
- RUSSIAN

Page 47
Words include: ant, anti, antic, con, cons, constitution, constitutional, count, cut, icon, icons, ins, ion, its, nit, nits, noun, out, tin, tins, tit, **unconstitutional**, uncut

Page 48
- ARIA
- WIDOW
- EULOGIZE
- SAGES (or RAGER)
- TAROT

▪ Solutions ▪

Page 49

Page 50

- V – colours of the rainbow: red, orange, yellow, green, blue, indigo, violet
- S – taxonomic classifications in increasing order of specificity: kingdom, phylum, class, order, family, genus, species
- FL – US state abbreviations in alphabetical order of state name: Alabama, Alaska, Arizona, Arkansas, California, Colorado, Connecticut, Delaware, Florida

Page 51

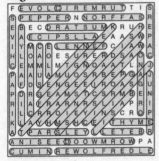

Page 52

- WAR and PEACE
- PRIDE and PREJUDICE
- CRIME and PUNISHMENT
- THE OLD MAN and THE SEA
- THE SOUND and THE FURY

Page 53

- ARES
- APOLLO
- HADES
- HERA
- ZEUS

Page 54

- *Death of a Salesman* by Arthur Miller
- *Romeo and Juliet* by William Shakespeare
- *A Streetcar Named Desire* by Tennessee Williams
- *Waiting for Godot* by Samuel Beckett
- *Pygmalion* by George Bernard Shaw

▪ Solutions ▪

Page 55

1 SKI
2 KISS
3 RISKS
4 SKIRTS
5 STRIKES
6 ASTERISK

Page 56

BACKLASH

SHOELACE

CERULEAN

ANACONDA

DAYDREAM

AMNESIAC

ACQUAINT

Page 57

```
S H A M P O O   A G O   A
O   R   E   R I P   R U G
P A C K A G E   P H I   A
  D   N   R       G U T
N U M E R I C   S K A   E
  L   E   D U M P   M
S T A S H   B   A M I S S
    T   O B I T   A   C
H   T A B   C H A N G E S
A P E       U   G   N
N   N U T   I G N O R E D
D U D   O W L   O   U   O
S   S I M   K I D N E Y S
```

Page 58

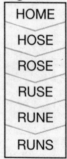

HOME	GALA
HOSE	GALL
ROSE	BALL
RUSE	BELL
RUNE	DELL
RUNS	DEAL

Page 59

- ELEPHANT
- ANTELOPE
- GIRAFFE
- RHINOCEROS
- ANTEATER

Page 60

The letters have been shifted back 5 places.

"Music expresses that which cannot be put into words and that which cannot remain silent."

– Victor Hugo

▪ Solutions ▪

Page 61

A	S	A	R	U	L	E		A	B	A	C	K
	E		E		I		H		A		E	
T	R	A	D	I	T	I	O	N	A	L	L	Y
	M		U		H		U		U		L	
C	O	U	N	S	E	L	S		M	E	A	L
	N		D				E		A		R	
		C	A	N	D	I	D	A	T	E		
	D		N		O				E	A		A
W	E	L	T		O	V	E	R	R	O	D	E
	F				W		L		I		I	V
S	E	L	F	M	O	T	I	V	A	T	E	D
	A		E		P		T		L		N	
S	T	R	E	W		D	E	N	S	I	T	Y

Page 62

- PEAR
- LIME
- APPLE
- ORANGE
- APRICOT

Page 63

Words include: aft, daft, deaf, default, **defaulted**, defeat, deflate, deflated, deft, elf, fad, fade, faded, fat, fate, fated, fault, faulted, feat, fed, fee, feed, feel, feet, felt, felted, feta, fete, feted, feud, feudal, feuded, flat, flea, fled, flee, fleet, flu, flue, flute, fluted, fuddle, fuel, leaf, leafed, left

Page 64

- CORN: POPCORN and CORNMEAL
- MARKET: SUPERMARKET and MARKETABLE
- ICE: OFFICE and ICEBOX
- TAN: SUNTAN and TANGOING
- THOUGHT: FORETHOUGHT and THOUGHTFULLY

Page 65

	C	A	P	A	C	I	T	A	N	C	E	
A		R		D		S		J		R		K
C	O	M	M	E	M	O	R	A	T	I	V	E
H		Q		M		R		R		T		Y
E	X	C	L	U	D	E	S		M	I	M	E
D		O		A		R		C		C		D
	U	N	I	T	Y		T	O	X	I	C	
S		F		E		B		R		Z		U
W	R	I	T		S	O	L	D	I	E	R	S
E		R		A		N		U				E
A	D	M	I	N	I	S	T	R	A	T	O	R
R		E		O		A		O		O		S
	I	D	E	N	T	I	F	Y	I	N	G	

Page 66

Inward 1 SWORN; **6** ORE; **9** HAVOC; **14** INAPT; **19** SET; **22** EDITS; **27** ORDERS; **33** ROTI; **37** NOMAD; **42** NEGATE; **48** NET

Outward 50 TENET; **45** AGENDA; **39** MONITORS; **31** RED; **28** ROSTI; **23** DETEST; **17** PANIC; **12** OVA; **9** HERON; **4** ROWS

▪ Solutions ▪

Page 67
- The letter 'm'
- The word 'short' – it becomes 'shorter' when you add 'e' and 'r' to the end

Page 68

	Y		U		W		U	
	O		N		A	W	R	Y
F	U	R	S		S	O	N	
	N	E	O	N		R		O
	G	E	L		E	K	E	D
P	E	K	I	N	G	E	S	E
	R		C		O	R	C	
		B	I	O				U
M	U	L	T	I	P	L	E	S
		E	E	L		E	V	E
T	E	D	D	Y	B	E	A	R

Page 69
- JUDO
- HOCKEY
- BOXING
- TENNIS
- BASKETBALL

Page 70
- EXODUS
- GENESIS
- ROMANS
- PSALMS
- NUMBERS

Page 71
Words include: ate, cat, cation, cations, cite, eta, exemplification, **exemplifications**, exit, feta, file, filet, fit, ion, ions, let, life, noise, sit, site, six

Page 72
- YUMMY
- TWIT
- ROAR
- PRIMP
- GULAG

▪ Solutions ▪

Page 73

Page 75

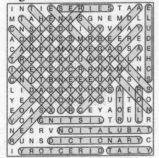

Page 77
- BRIE
- CHEDDAR
- EDAM
- FETA
- GOUDA

Page 74
- O – elements in increasing atomic number: Hydrogen, Helium, Lithium, Beryllium, Boron, Carbon, Nitrogen, Oxygen
- Monarchs of the United Kingdom going back in time: Elizabeth II, George VI, Edward VIII, George V, Edward VII, Victoria, William IV, George IV, George III, George II, George I, Anne
- TND – James Bond film titles in reverse chronological order: *Spectre, Skyfall, Quantum of Solace, Casino Royale, Die Another Day, The World is Not Enough, Tomorrow Never Dies*

Page 76
- BACON and EGGS
- MEAT and POTATOES
- MACARONI and CHEESE
- CHEESE and CRACKERS
- STRAWBERRIES and CREAM

Page 78
- *Mona Lisa* by Leonardo da Vinci
- *The Starry Night* by Vincent Van Gogh
- *The Birth Of Venus* by Sandro Botticelli
- *Girl With a Pearl Earring* by Johannes Vermeer
- *The Kiss* by Gustav Klimt

▪ Solutions ▪

Page 79
1 DOE
2 DOVE
3 VIDEO
4 DEVOID
5 OVERDID
6 DIVORCED

Page 80
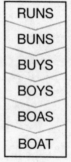

TIRAMISU

SUBURBAN

ANYWHERE

REHEARSE

SEQUOIAS

ASTONISH

SHEPHERD

Page 81

Page 82

RUNS
BUNS
BUYS
BOYS
BOAS
BOAT

DEAL
PEAL
PEAK
PERK
PORK
WORK

Page 83
- MARTINI
- MANHATTAN
- COSMOPOLITAN
- LONG ISLAND ICED TEA
- WHITE RUSSIAN

Page 84
The letters have been shifted forward 7 places.

"You can never cross the ocean until you have the courage to lose sight of the shore."

– Christopher Columbus

▪ Solutions ▪

Page 85

Page 86

- DEGAS
- RAPHAEL
- TITIAN
- DA VINCI
- GIOTTO

Page 87

Words include: age, aged, ago, argot, dog, dotage, drag, ego, erg, ergo, fog, forage, foraged, forge, forged, forget, frog, gad, gate, gated, gather, gear, get, goad, goat, goatherd, **godfather**, gore, gored, got, grade, graft, grafted, grate, grated, great, hag, hog, ogre, rag, rage, raged, tag, toga

Page 88

- SEED: BIRDSEED and SEEDLESS
- CRAFTS: SPACECRAFTS and CRAFTSMAN
- WOOD: DRIFTWOOD and WOODCHUCK
- HAND: FREEHAND and HANDCUFFED
- WED: VIEWED and WEDLOCK

Page 89

Page 90

Inward 1 PASTE; **6** LLAMA; **11** CAP; **14** LABEL; **19** ECLAIR; **25** TRAPPING; **33** NIT; **36** TODDLE; **42** WRIST; **47** RATS

Outward 50 START; **45** SIR; **42** WELD; **38** DOTTING; **31** NIP; **28** PAR; **25** TRIAL; **20** CELEB; **15** ALPACA; **9** MALLET; **3** SAP

179

▪ Solutions ▪

Page 91
- Yesterday, today and tomorrow
- A 'b'

Page 92

	S		B		W		G	
	Q		A		A	G	O	G
F	U	L	L	T	I	L	T	
	E	A	T		F	O	O	D
	E	X	I	T		S	T	Y
	Z		C			S	H	E
P	I	N		V		Y	E	S
	N	O	S	E	S		D	
	G	O	A	T		T	O	T
		S	I	S		A	G	E
P	E	E	L		M	U	S	E

Page 93
- TOKYO
- LONDON
- ATHENS
- MOSCOW
- BEIJING

Page 94
- MOZART
- BEETHOVEN
- CHOPIN
- SCHUBERT
- VIVALDI

Page 95
Words include: criming, disc, discriminating, gnat, man, mas, mat, mating, nit, rim, riming, sang, sat, satin, sating, sir, sit, siting, tam, taming, tan, tang, tin, ting, **undiscriminating**

Page 96
- SHUNS
- DICED
- AURA
- BEDAUB
- MEDIUM

▪ Solutions ▪

Page 97

A	Q	U	A	T	I	C		P	I	C
U		N		H		H		S		R
T	I	C		E	X	O	T	I	C	A
H		L		Y		R				F
O	V	A	L		S	A	C	H	E	T
R		S		S		L		U		S
I	M	P	A	I	R		K	N	O	W
Z				E		I		D		O
I	N	J	U	R	E	D		R	U	M
N		A		R		E		E		A
G	Y	M		A	B	A	N	D	O	N

Page 99

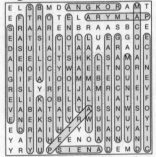

Page 101

- ASH
- BEECH
- OAK
- PINE
- WILLOW

Page 98

- E – numbers: one, two, three, four, five, six, seven, eight
- AJ – US presidents in order: George Washington, John Adams, Thomas Jefferson, James Madison, James Monroe, John Adams, Andrew Jackson
- TLB – *Chronicles of Narnia* titles in story chronology order: *The Magician's Nephew*; *The Lion, the Witch and the Wardrobe*; *The Horse and His Boy*; *Prince Caspian*; *The Voyage of the Dawn Treader*; *The Silver Chair*; *The Last Battle*

Page 100

- SIMON and GARFUNKEL
- HALL and OATES
- SONNY and CHER
- LENNON and MCCARTNEY
- IKE and TINA

Page 102

- *Moby-Dick* by Herman Melville
- *Jane Eyre* by Charlotte Bronte
- *I Know Why the Caged Bird Sings* by Maya Angelou
- *Mrs. Dalloway* by Virginia Woolf
- *The Great Gatsby* by F. Scott Fitzgerald

▪ Solutions ▪

Page 103

1 YAP
2 PRAY
3 SPRAY
4 REPAYS
5 PLAYERS
6 SPARSELY

Page 104

| F | U | C | H | S | I | A | S |

| A | S | S | E | M | B | L | E |

| L | E | M | O | N | A | D | E |

| D | E | C | I | S | I | V | E |

| V | E | G | A | N | I | S | M |

| S | M | A | R | T | E | S | T |

| S | T | U | T | T | E | R | S |

Page 105

```
S T A C K S     T   D I P
  O   U   A   M E N U   E
B U R R I T O   N   E G G
  G     C   B U S     U
C H O R I Z O   E M A I L
A   W   N   E       O   L
M A N A G E   W E A L T H
  U   Y     I   V   E   O
U R G E S   B E A R I N G
  A       C H I D     E
A S K   O   S H E L T E R
R   I R O N   E   I   D
T U T   P   M O D E S T
```

Page 106

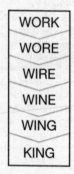

Page 107

- ISAAC NEWTON
- ALBERT EINSTEIN
- THOMAS EDISON
- MARIE CURIE
- ADA LOVELACE

Page 108

The letters have been shifted forward 10 places.

"You cannot escape the responsibility of tomorrow by evading it today."

– Abraham Lincoln

▪ Solutions ▪

Page 109

Page 110
- LETTUCE
- LEEK
- KALE
- SWEET POTATO
- ONION

Page 111
Words include: den, denim, dent, dew, die, diet, dim, dime, dimer, dimwit, din, dine, diner, dint, dire, dirt, drew, edit, end, mend, mid, **midwinter**, mind, mined, minted, mired, mitred, red, remind, rend, rewind, rid, ride, rimed, rind, tend, tide, tidier, tied, timed, timid, timider, tinder, tined, tired, trend, tried, twined, wed, weird, wend, wide, widen, wider, wind, windier, wined, wired

Page 112
- LOIN: SIRLOIN and LOINCLOTH
- SLEEP: OVERSLEEP and SLEEPLESS
- BOY: PLAYBOY and BOYFRIEND
- POST: SIGNPOST and POSTAGE
- BREAD: CORNBREAD and BREADWINNER

Page 113

Page 114
Inward 1 TABLES; **7** AERIAL; **13** RAMPANT; **20** LAX; **23** EXISTS; **29** GNASH; **34** TURTLE; **40** BILLION; **47** WARD

Outward 50 DRAWN; **45** OIL; **42** LIBEL; **37** TRUTHS; **31** ANGST; **26** SIX; **23** EXALT; **18** NAP; **15** MAR; **12** LAIR; **8** EASEL; **3** BAT

▪ Solutions ▪

Page 115
- Hamlet's uncle Claudius, because he did murder most foul/fowl
- Silence

Page 116

	P		E		R		S	
	L		M		O	D	E	S
A	U	T	O		N	E	W	
	M	E	T	E		V		W
	P	R	I	O	R	I	T	Y
	E	R	O	S		C	U	E
G	R	I	N		W	E	B	
		F	A	R				B
	O	I	L		B	E	A	U
		E	L	D	E	R	L	Y
R	O	S	Y		D	A	I	S

Page 117
- JUNK
- YACHT
- FERRY
- CANOE
- CATAMARAN

Page 118
- PORK
- SALAMI
- CHICKEN
- MUTTON
- VENISON

Page 119
Words include: air, aping, appropriating, map, mas, **misappropriating**, mop, moping, nip, nit, omit, pair, pas, pat, pin, pit, pita, pop, pro, prom, prop, roping, sap, sin, sing, tap, taping, timing, tin, ting, tip

Page 120
- MINIM
- EVADE
- RECUR
- GLUING
- EWE

▪ Solutions ▪

Page 121

T	A	C	K	L	E		J	A	M	S
O		A		A		A		I		H
P	E	R		R	E	S	O	L	V	E
A		I		V		K				E
Z	E	B	R	A		S	W	E	E	P
		O				M				
F	O	U	N	D		E	X	P	E	L
E				E		Q		L		O
T	A	B	L	E	A	U		O	R	B
C		A		P		A		Y		B
H	I	D	E		G	L	O	S	S	Y

Page 123

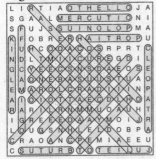

Page 122

- E – fractions in decreasing size: half, third, quarter, fifth, sixth, seventh, eighth
- P – Star signs: Aries, Taurus, Gemini, Cancer, Leo, Virgo, Libra, Scorpio, Sagittarius, Capricorn, Aquarius, Pisces
- GR – *The Twelve Days of Christmas* gifts in descending order: Drummers Drumming, Pipers Piping, Lords a-Leaping, Ladies Dancing, Maids a-Milking, Swans a-Swimming, Geese a-Laying, Gold Rings

Page 124

- ABOVE and BEYOND
- BAIT and SWITCH
- HIGH and DRY
- LIVE and LEARN
- NOW and AGAIN

Page 125

BED

CHAIR

SOFA

STOOL

TABLE

Page 126

- *The Raven* by Edgar Allan Poe
- *If* by Rudyard Kipling
- *I Wandered Lonely As A Cloud* by William Wordsworth
- *The Road Not Taken* by Robert Frost
- *Do Not Go Gentle Into That Good Night* by Dylan Thomas

▪ Solutions ▪

Page 127

1 RID
2 BIRD
3 BRIDE
4 DEBRIS
5 BINDERS
6 BRANDIES

Page 128

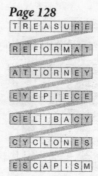

TREASURE

REFORMAT

ATTORNEY

EYEPIECE

CELIBACY

CYCLONES

ESCAPISM

Page 129

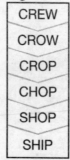

Page 130

CREW
CROW
CROP
CHOP
SHOP
SHIP

KING
KIND
FIND
FOND
FORD
LORD

Page 131

- DRACULA
- OLIVER TWIST
- FRANKENSTEIN
- LITTLE WOMEN
- WUTHERING HEIGHTS

Page 132

The letters have been shifted backward 7 places.

"No man, for any considerable period, can wear one face to himself and another to the multitude, without finally getting bewildered as to which may be the true."

– Nathaniel Hawthorne

▪ Solutions ▪

Page 133

Page 134

- CARMEN
- ORPHEUS
- SWAN LAKE
- THE NUTCRACKER
- THE RITE OF SPRING

Page 135

Words include: amp, amply, apiary, damp, damply, dip, drip, imp, impala, imply, lamp, lap, lapidary, limp, lip, map, pad, paid, pail, pair, pal, palm, palmy, par, parlay, pay, plaid, play, ply, pram, pray, prim, primal, primly, pry, pyramid, **pyramidal**, ramp, rap, rapid, rapidly, rip, yap, yip

Page 136

- PATH: WARPATH and PATHWAY
- JOYS: OVERJOYS and JOYSTICK
- PLANK: GANGPLANK and PLANKTON
- TABLE: TIMETABLE and TABLETOP
- VAN: MINIVAN and VANGUARD

Page 137

Page 138

Inward 1 TRACES; **7** IRE;
10 CRIME; **15** ACROSS;
21 END; **24** AMIGO;
29 YIELD; **34** ERE; **37** DROOP;
42 METRO; **47** TARO

Outward 50 ORATOR;
44 TEMPO; **39** ORDERED;
32 LEI; **29** YOGI;
25 MADNESS; **18** ORCA;
14 EMIR; **10** CERISE; **4** CART

▪ Solutions ▪

Page 139
- The word 'wholesome'
- It comes in the middle of every 'day'

Page 140

	R	R		W		P	
	A	E		A	B	U	T
O	V	U	M		G	Y	M
	I	M	A	M		A	I	M
	O	A	R		O	N	C	E
	L	K			D	E	W
M	I	A		P	A	L	
	V		O		A	N	D
S	M	A	C	K		R	O	E
	O		R	E	I	G	N	S
O	B	E	Y	S		E	E	K

Page 141
- LILY
- ROSE
- TULIP
- VIOLET
- LAVENDER

Page 142
- NAAN
- BAGEL
- TORTILLA
- BAGUETTE
- PUMPERNICKEL

Page 143
Words include: apprehensive, **apprehensiveness**, apse, ass, eve, even, evens, eves, hen, hens, her, nee, pas, pass, passe, sap, saps, see, seen, seven, sevens, she, sheen, spa, spas, vie

Page 144
- DUPED
- ACACIA
- EAVE
- GASBAG
- WALLOW

▪ Solutions ▪

Page 145

Page 146

- S – months: February, March, April, May, June, July, August, September
- LA – Summer Olympic venues going back in time: Rio de Janeiro, London, Beijing, Athens, Sydney, Atlanta, Barcelona, Seoul, Los Angeles
- PD – *Doctor Who* actors in reverse order: Jodie Whittaker, Peter Capaldi, Matt Smith, David Tennant, Christopher Eccleston, Paul McGann, Sylvester McCoy, Colin Baker, Peter Davison

Page 147

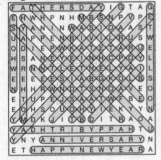

Page 148

- TRINIDAD and TOBAGO
- BOSNIA and HERZEGOVINA
- ANTIGUA and BARBUDA
- SAINT KITTS and NEVIS
- SÃO TOMÉ AND PRÍNCIPE

Page 149

- BRAIN
- HEART
- LIVER
- LUNG
- SKIN

Page 150

- *Billie Jean* by Michael Jackson
- *Back To Black* by Amy Winehouse
- *Take On Me* by A-Ha
- *No Woman, No Cry* by Bob Marley
- *Another One Bites the Dust* by Queen

▪ Solutions ▪

Page 151
1 GNU
2 SUNG
3 USING
4 GENIUS
5 ENSUING
6 PENGUINS

Page 152
GRAFFITI

TITANIUM

UMBRELLA

LAVISHLY

LYRICIST

STUDIOUS

USURPERS

Page 153
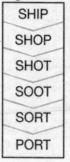

Page 154
| SHIP |
| SHOP |
| SHOT |
| SOOT |
| SORT |
| PORT |

| LORD |
| LORN |
| LOON |
| NOON |
| NEON |
| PEON |

Page 155
- PSYCHO
- CASABLANCA
- THE GODFATHER
- GOODFELLAS
- GONE WITH THE WIND

Page 156
The letters have been shifted forward 9 places.

"I would always rather be happy than dignified."
                        – Charlotte Bronte

▪ Solutions ▪

Page 157

Page 158

- DIAMOND
- EMERALD
- JADE
- GARNET
- OPAL

Page 159

Words include: enlist, inlet, inlets, insult, isle, islet, lei, leis, lens, lent, lest, let, lets, lie, lies, lieu, line, liner, liners, lines, lint, lints, lire, list, listen, lit, litre, litres, litter, litters, lure, lures, lust, lustier, lustre, lute, lutes, nil, nils, result, rile, riles, rule, rules, rustle, silent, silt, slier, slit, slitter, slue, slur, stile, sunlit, tile, tiles, tilt, tilts, tinsel, title, titles, **turnstile**, turtle, turtles, until, untiles, utensil

Page 160

- DOG: BULLDOG and DOGMAS
- DRUM: EARDRUM and DRUMSTICK
- MILL: TREADMILL and MILLION
- LOG: BACKLOG and LOGJAM
- JUST: READJUST and JUSTICE

Page 161

```
■ R E Q U E S T ■ M O J O
M ■ L ■ R ■ C ■ A ■ O ■
A D O R N ■ A N O R A K S
T ■ Q ■ S ■ L ■ R ■ E ■
C R U X ■ L A Z I N E S S
H ■ E ■ B ■ R ■ G ■ N ■
■ K N E A D ■ B I B L E ■
C ■ C ■ N ■ F ■ N ■ I ■ P
E V E R Y D A Y ■ E G G S
O ■ O ■ A ■ L ■ C ■ H ■ A
E T E R N A L ■ H O T E L
E ■ A ■ E ■ E ■ O ■ E ■ M
E D G Y ■ K N O W I N G ■
```

Page 162

Inward 1 PILES; **6** NESTLE;
12 BLISS; **17** OFFER;
22 DOGMA; **27** MIXING;
33 NIL; **36** RADIO;
41 KRONA; **46** MEMOS
Outward 50 SOME;
46 MANOR; **41** KOI;
38 DARLING; **31** NIX;
28 IMAM; **24** GOD; **21** REF;
18 FOSSIL; **12** BELT; **8** SENSE;
3 LIP

▪ Solutions ▪

Page 163

- 'Anyone', since then you have only 'one' left (alternative answers include begone, bygone, debone, intone, ketone, redone, rezone, throne and undone)
- The word 'noise', when it loses an I/eye

Page 165

- RED
- BLACK
- NORTH
- BALTIC
- CASPIAN

Page 164

	A	V		F		A		
	D	E	A	D	L	O	S	S
B	O	R	N		A		S	
		R		U	M	B	E	R
	P		H		B	A	S	H
F	I	G	U	R	E	D		O
	C	A	R		A		S	
		B	R	O	U	G	H	T
R	A	B	I	D		L	I	E
		L	E	D		U	P	S
S	E	E	D		V	E	S	T